MIND AEROBICS:

The FundaMENTALS
of
Memory Fitness

by Phil Bruschi

A MIND AEROBICS PUBLICATION
P.O. Box 11233
Yardville, New Jersey 08620

MIND AEROBICS: The FundaMENTALS of Memory Fitness
by Phil Bruschi

Copyright © 1997
A MIND AEROBICS Publication
Printed in the United States of America

ISBN   0-9656555-0-4

Credits:
Book Design: Mary Salerno
Cover Design: Mary Salerno & Eric Housel
Editor: Robin K. Levinson
Illustrations: Eric Housel
Logo: Frank Cirillo
Photo (back cover): Michael Mancuso

To my wife, Barbara

ACKNOWLEDGMENTS

I would like to express my sincere appreciation and gratitude to those who have helped in the completion of this book. In particular, I am grateful to my wife, Barbara, for her wisdom, creative ideas, and endless hours of labor on this project. My editor, Robin Levinson, who took the multitude of information and organized it with clarity of purpose. I am also indebted to Mary Salerno for her talent, knowledge, and excellent technological skills in formatting this book. Thanks to Eric Housel for his illustrations which visually enhanced the book's concepts.

I am grateful to Janet Haney and Judy Pavano for their hours of assistance in reading through this manuscript and providing useful comments. Heartfelt appreciation is extended to Carol Kivler and Nick Corcodilos for their guidance and encouragement for my taking on this endeavor.

Finally, I would like to thank my family for their understanding and support, especially my daughters, Dana and Marcy, for letting me hide out in my office all those hours.

PREFACE

Although the concept of memory enhancement is nothing new, the last five years have seen a resurgence of research in the memory field. This renewed interest comes on the heels of new technology that allows scientists to visualize the brain at work. As a result, a number of books about memory have been published in recent years. Unfortunately for the lay person, most are technical in nature, focusing on brain biology, memory theories, and research findings. *MIND AEROBICS: The FundaMENTALS of Memory Fitness* is different. It is a practical, down-to-earth guide to understanding and improving your memory—both on and off the job. If you involve yourself totally in the pages that follow, this book can lead you through a powerful journey toward self-discovery.

The title of this book—*MIND AEROBICS*—reinforces the fact that exercising your brain strengthens your mental abilities, just as exercising your body makes your muscles stronger. The memory-building activities presented in Part Three of this book will challenge and stimulate your brain. Most people are astonished to realize how much untapped memory potential they have. In an increasingly technological and complex world, it has never been more important to develop your memory skills to their fullest.

Tips and techniques designed to improve your short- and long-term memory are major components of *MIND AEROBICS*. But as you will see, *MIND AEROBICS* also emphasizes exploring your current understanding of your memory's capabilities, and how various outside influences, such as exercise and nutrition, bear on your memory fitness.

MIND AEROBICS is written in a self-paced, interactive format. By reading the book with pencil in hand, you will be able to do the various exercises and assessments as you encounter them. Another way of making the most of this book is reading it in an environment that is conducive to effective concentration.

From my perspective, *MIND AEROBICS* can be used in a variety of ways:

- <u>Self-Instruction</u>. Everyone has memory strengths and weaknesses. By completing the exercises and activities in this book, you will discover yours. More importantly, you will acquire the skills you need to turn your weaknesses into strengths and make your strengths even stronger. All you need is an open mind and a willingness to practice new skills.

- <u>Seminars and Workshops</u>. Educators and trainers who work in the memory-enhancement field can use this book as a text. By distributing *MIND AEROBICS* to students/participants at the start of a class or workshop, teachers or trainers can refer them to sections, exercises, or assessments that are pertinent to the lesson at hand. This book can also be used to develop lesson plans and training outlines.

- <u>Presentations or Informal Study Groups</u>. This book contains everything you need to present the topic of "memory enhancement" at an informal, "brown bag" study group session.

- <u>Reference Material</u>. Once you've completed all the activities and exercises in *MIND AEROBICS*, keep the volume on your bookshelf. It will serve as an excellent reference source that can be easily reviewed from time to time.

Regardless of how you use this book, be assured that its information, tips, techniques, and strategies have benefited thousands of people.

Contents

The mind is like a muscle. If it is constantly challenged with new learning, it grows stronger; if not, it weakens.

– Howard Gardner

PART ONE

KEEP AN OPEN MIND TO GET STARTED

We act on our beliefs. Some people believe they have excellent memory skills; they can remember almost everyone they've ever met and everything they've ever read. At the other end of the spectrum are those who believe they are stuck with a bad memory and that there is nothing they can do about it. They forget people's names seconds after they are introduced. When reading a novel, they often find themselves rereading sentences or whole paragraphs just to stay abreast of the plot.

Memory Myths

I believe that everyone has the capacity to vastly improve their memory skills. After reading this chapter, it is my hope that you will, too. The key is believing in your own potential. If you always expect to forget people's names, it will become a self-fulfilling prophecy. If you, instead, acknowledge that you are weak in the area of recalling names and need to work on that skill, you are already halfway home. The notion that some people are stuck with poor memories is one of several memory myths that can hold you back from making real improvements. Here are some more:

Myth #1: We normally use a high percentage of our brain's capacity.

On the contrary, experts estimate that most people use a mere 1 to 20 percent of their brain's potential. That means at least 80 percent of our brains may do little more than take up space. Imagine how much more we could accomplish by increasing the amount of brain power we use to 25 percent, 50 percent, or higher. I believe we all have this potential, which is why I spend so much time teaching, motivating, and training people to sharpen their memory skills. By sharpening your memory, you are sharpening your mind.

Myth #2: Some people are simply born with better memory skills.

Memory is primarily a learned skill. Heredity undoubtedly plays some role in how well our brains retain information, but education and experience are far more important. Instead of classifying memory skills as "good" or "bad," it is more accurate to say a person's memory is either "trained" or "untrained."

Myth #3: There is a secret to developing a good memory.

It is easy to assume that there is a secret or trick to improving your memory. In reality, there is no "quick fix" or single tool that will help you remember something. In order to improve your memory, you must be willing to learn and use a variety of techniques. With practice, the set of skills laid out in this book will have you performing memory feats that your untrained mind couldn't begin to accomplish.

Myth #4: There is an easy way to remember things.

Remembering things consistently and accurately takes work. Most people learn to remember through rote, or repetition. Rote memorization doesn't necessarily get easier with practice because you are always trying to remember something new. The memory techniques and strategies I will offer you will probably be difficult at first. But with practice, they can become second nature. It is important to be patient with yourself. In some instances, you may need to take two steps backward before taking a step forward.

Myth #5: The older you get, the more difficult it becomes to develop a better memory and sharper mind.

While changes do occur in the brain as people age, senility is not a normal part of the aging process. Older people who challenge themselves intellectually and do mental exercises can keep their minds and memories sharp. It is not unusual to come across individuals who have done their best work in their fifties or sixties. Learning can continue well into your later years provided you have a healthy mind and a positive outlook on life.

Myth #6: Hearing and listening are the same process.

There are significant differences between hearing and listening. Hearing is the physical process that is triggered when sound waves hit your eardrums. Listening, like memorizing, is largely a learned skill. A vital component of listening is paying attention. Paying attention—the first step in the process of storing information in your long-term memory—requires a conscious decision. By deciding to pay attention, you are focusing on what you need to remember. We sometimes think we have forgotten something, when, in fact, we never really listened and learned it in the first place. Forgetting is often not a <u>retention</u> problem but an <u>attention</u> problem.

Myth #7: Attitude has nothing to do with memory.

Attitude has everything to do with improving your memory, and, for that matter, accomplishing anything in life. People who say, "I have a terrible memory for names," or "Remind me to call, or I'll forget," have talked themselves into being forgetful. In most cases, if you think you can't remember, you won't remember. Or, as Henry Ford put it: "Whether you think you can or whether you think you can't, you're right." By embracing a "can-do" attitude toward memory enhancement, you are more likely to succeed.

Myth #8: Nutrition has no real relationship to memory.

Here's a little food for thought: Nutrition and diet can enhance or hinder your ability to concentrate and remember. Certain foods increase the production and function of chemicals in the brain that are directly involved with helping us concentrate. The brain absorbs proteins, carbohydrates, vitamins, and minerals from the blood and turns them into the chemicals used to learn, think, feel, and remember. For instance, eating protein-rich foods (broccoli, green beans, fish, eggs, veal, etc.) before times when peak performance is required can prevent fatigue. For example, if you have three meetings in the afternoon, eat vegetables with protein at lunch and avoid processed sugars, which give you an immediate lift but rapidly bring you down.

Myth #9: Having too much to remember can clutter the mind and cause confusion.

Information overload is not the real reason we have trouble remembering things. How much you remember depends on how you mentally organize information as it is given to you. Consider a library, which holds a mind-boggling amount of information. It is the library's organization that makes it possible to find anything. The brain works in a similar way. Memory is based on association. As information comes into the long-term memory, ideally it is stored according to subject matter. That's why the more you learn about a particular subject, the easier it becomes to learn even more about that subject.

Myth #10: Physical activity and memory have nothing to do with each other.

Aristotle once said, "The mind and body must be one." The healthier your body is, the healthier your mind will be. Numerous scientific studies have shown that physical activity and exercise can often alleviate depression and reduce anxiety. Exercising regularly can also improve mental function, social skills, and self-image. All of these affect memory.

Benefits of Memory Enhancement

People have their own, unique reasons for improving their memory. An insurance salesperson may wish to impress his customers by remembering where their children were attending college. A caterer may need to remember recipes she tries while traveling abroad. A grandmother wants to remember her grandchildren's birthdays. Regardless of your motivation to improve your memory, the benefits have far-reaching effects, both personally and professionally. In some cases, the ability to remember details can actually determine whether you succeed or fail in business. Knowing this, it is easy to motivate yourself to improve your memory skills.

EXERCISE 1-1: TARGETING YOUR MEMORY GOALS

List below as many personal and professional benefits as you can think of—both big and small—for improving your memory. Be as specific as possible. There are no right and wrong answers.

Here are the most common reasons for improving memory that have been cited by countless people I have trained over the last 20 years.

PERSONAL BENEFITS

- Confidence increases. This happens each time you experience a memory success.

- Stress and anxiety are reduced. Remembering things with less effort frees up your mind for further recall.

- You become more organized. This, in turn, helps you meet deadlines.

- You become more creative and imaginative. Memory-enhancement techniques require you to enhance these aspects of your mind.

- Social relationships improve. When you meet new people, you'll have less trouble remembering their names and details about their lives.

- You become a better conversationalist. An enhanced memory heightens your mental agility, learning power, and conversation skills.

- You have less trouble remembering dates, doctor's appointments, birthdays, anniversaries, phone numbers, and the like.

- Your concentration habits improve as you learn to be a better listener. This will help you learn faster and retain more information.

PROFESSIONAL BENEFITS

- You become more observant of what's going on around you. Paying closer attention to detail makes you safer in your physical environment. It also can make you more astute on the job.

- You have less difficulty remembering important details of current work projects and assignments. This will make you a more valued employee.

- You will remember more clients' names and faces. This can directly improve your bottom line.

- You eliminate more careless errors by focusing on the most important points to be remembered.

- You become a more effective problem solver and decision maker.

- You make more effective presentations or speeches without fear of forgetting salient points.

- You retain and recall more information gleaned from meetings and training sessions.

- You improve your ability to follow instructions from supervisors.

- You enhance the professional image projected by you and your company. Impressing a client by remembering his name and specific needs, for example, reflects positively on you and the whole company.

EXERCISE 1-2: YOUR MEMORY PROFILE

The self-assessment below is designed to provide you with feedback about your beliefs, attitudes, and behaviors regarding your memory. It will help you identify areas of strength and those in need of improvement. Instructions: Place a check beside all the statements that apply to you most of the time. Be as candid as possible.

_____   1. I seek out opportunities to learn and challenge my mind as I get older.

_____   2. I give my undivided attention to what a speaker is saying.

_____   3. I look for ways to stimulate my mind, personally and professionally.

_____   4. I am receptive to using new memory strategies and systems to organize information I need to remember.

_____   5. I look at physical exercise as being beneficial to my mind as well as my body.

_____   6. I project a positive attitude about my mind and memory abilities.

_____   7. I am able to overcome any internal or external distractions when someone is talking to me.

_____   8. I seek out problem-solving tasks that challenge my mind and memory.

_____   9. I am open-minded to trying memory techniques, even if they seem silly or illogical.

_____   10. I make physical exercise one of my priorities.

_____   11. I use memory aids to help me remember things.

_____   12. I use all my senses to take in what is going on around me.

_____   13. I seek out as many learning and training opportunities as I can.

Continued on next page

_____ 14. I approach tasks creatively and believe in using my imagination to solve problems.

_____ 15. I believe exercising my body on a regular basis is more important than how intensely I exercise.

_____ 16. I don't expect my memory to be perfect all the time.

_____ 17. I discipline myself to be attentive and concentrate even when I am not motivated.

_____ 18. I play games that exercise my mind, such as crossword puzzles, Scrabble, chess, and Jeopardy.

_____ 19. I learn best by seeing and reading.

_____ 20. I acknowledge the psychological benefits of regular physical activity.

_____ 21. I look for ways to improve my memory skills.

_____ 22. I am aware of how diet can influence my ability to concentrate.

_____ 23. I read detective or mystery books.

_____ 24. I try to remember information by picturing it in my mind.

_____ 25. I realize that regular physical exercise improves my mental acuity.

SCORING

Self-confidence: 1, 6, 11, 16, 21

Attention/Concentration: 2, 7, 12, 17, 22

Mind Activity: 3, 8, 13, 18, 23

Visualization/Association/Imagination: 4, 9, 14, 19, 24

Physical Activity: 5, 10, 15, 20, 25

Each category above (self-confidence, attention/concentration, etc.) corresponds to one of the five fundaMENTALS described on the next page. The numbers following each category correspond to the statements above. Take a few minutes now to note the number of checks you have in each category. The more checks you have for each category, the stronger you are in that particular area. Consider any category with three or fewer checks an area you need to work on. Don't be discouraged if you don't have as many checks as you would like. It's been my experience that most people can improve to some degree in most areas. So, let's get started.

The Five FundaMENTALS
of Memory Fitness

Every day, scientists acquire new insights into how we remember. They are discovering that the development of our mental powers depends on everything from the foods we eat to the way we exercise our minds and bodies. To help you make the most of the current research, the *MIND AEROBICS* approach offers five fundaMENTALS of memory enhancement. They are:

1. <u>Improve your self-concept</u>. Before you can improve your memory, you must first believe you can do it. In Part Two, you will find a variety of exercises designed to assess and improve your self-concept about your memory potential.

2. <u>Increase your powers of attention and concentration</u>. Most memory lapses can be traced to poor listening skills. In Part Two, you will learn how to improve your ability to listen, comprehend, and remember.

3. <u>Keep your mind active</u>. Just as your muscles need regular physical activity to stay toned, your brain must be frequently stimulated and challenged in order to operate at peak efficiency. Part Three offers a wide range of techniques designed to keep your mind active.

4. <u>Use visualization, association, and imagination</u>. How good your memory is depends largely on the acuity of your "mind's eye." In Part Three, you will encounter many techniques to improve these so-called "right brain" powers.

5. <u>Adopt a lifestyle of physical fitness</u>. A healthy body and a healthy mind are inextricably linked. In Part Four, you will find out why. You will also find tips that can help you make exercise a part of your lifestyle.

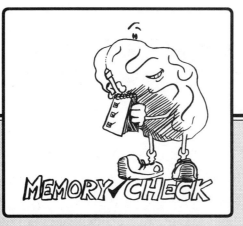

In the space below, write down the most important points you learned from Part One (e.g., some myths and facts, *MIND AEROBICS* FundaMENTALS, or something you learned from your memory profile). The mere act of writing things down will help you transfer information from your short-term to long-term memory.

_____

_____

_____

_____

_____

_____

_____

_____

_____

_____

_____

_____

_____

_____

_____

Be sure you exercise to optimize!

PART TWO

HOW MEMORY WORKS

Although many aspects of the human brain are still a mystery, there are several things scientists agree on regarding memory. Perhaps the most basic widely accepted concept is that the memory process consists of three distinct stages: sensory, short-term, and long-term memory.

The Three Stages of Memory

SENSORY MEMORY. At the sensory stage, you become aware of information through one or more of your senses—hearing, seeing, touching, smelling, tasting. But because your senses are constantly bombarded with stimuli, a great deal of what they take in is immediately discarded by your brain. For example, the image of a neon "Hotel" sign seen from the window of a moving car typically lasts just a second or two in your sensory memory. Unless there is a reason for that sign to enter your short-term memory, you will not remember ever having seen it. If, however, that sign triggers an emotion or recollection from your long-term memory, or it is otherwise significant to you, it enters the second stage of memory, short-term.

SHORT-TERM MEMORY. A stimulus enters your short-term memory when you focus your attention on it. If, for example, that neon "Hotel" sign was a landmark you had been looking for, the sight of it will grab your attention and enter your short-term memory. Focusing your attention on one thing means that you are diverting your attention from almost everything else.

Because we must be selective in where we focus our attention at any given moment, the vast majority of the sights, sounds, smells, and other stimuli we are exposed to never enters the short-term memory and is therefore not usually available for recall later. For instance, a college student whose mind wanders during lectures probably has a tough time recalling information during a test. As mentioned earlier, most instances of forgetfulness stem from failing to pay attention.

Short-term memory can also be equated with conscious thought. In essence, you make a conscious decision of what you would like to place in your short-term memory. A common example is repeating a phone number to yourself several times after calling directory assistance. As soon as you dial the number, you allow it to evaporate from your short-term memory. What you decide to put in your short-term memory is a matter of personal interest. Your interests may change as you get older, but you continue to store selected information in your short-term memory throughout life, provided your mind remains healthy.

This second stage of memory has a limited storage capability. Many experts believe the short-term memory can hold no more than six to nine items or bits of information—such as the digits in a phone number—at any given time. As exemplified by briefly remembering a phone number, not all information that registers in short-term memory gets transferred to long-term memory. The information in your short-term memory will be forgotten in about 10 seconds unless continual repetition of the information takes place or it is transferred to long-term memory through one of the association techniques discussed later in this book.

LONG-TERM MEMORY. This final stage of memory is virtually limitless in its capacity to store information. Your long-term memory can hold as much as one-quadrillion separate bits of information over the course of a lifetime. Put another way, you could fill the World Trade Center's twin towers from top to bottom with stacks of information, and you would still have room in your long-term memory to store more information. This is why the long-term memory is sometimes referred to as "the knowledge bank." Information in your long-term memory can be as recent as the person you met a minute ago or as old as a trauma that happened when you were three. If learned well in the first place and provided your brain is still healthy, information in long-term memory is available for recall until the day you die.

To improve your memory, you simply need to increase your ability to move information from short-term to long-term memory. You do this by making better decisions about how to place information into your knowledge bank. The next time you learn something new, ask yourself some of the following questions:

- Would I like to remember this particular piece of information?
- How meaningful is the information to me?
- How is this information organized as I absorb it?
- How can I link this new information to previous knowledge?

- Which association (mnemonic) strategies can I use? (These will be discussed in Part Three.)

- How can I use all of my senses to take in this information?

How We Remember

We remember through a process known as the "encoding and retrieval system."

ENCODING. Encoding is the act of putting information into our long-term memory. A number of mental tasks are involved here. The first is paying attention, or making a conscious effort to focus on what you need to remember. The next is association, or connecting that new information with relevant information that already exists in your long-term memory. For the most part associating is done unconsciously, but it can also be done deliberately. When association is deliberate, there is a greater likelihood that the new information will be committed to long-term memory and recalled later with greater ease.

The final step in the encoding process is elaboration. Elaboration determines how much detail is being committed to memory, or the depth at which the information is to be stored. It means making more mental connections and further organizing the new information so that it becomes embedded in your long-term memory with as much accuracy as possible. Later in Part Two and in Part Three, you will learn a variety of techniques to ensure that information you wish to remember is properly encoded.

RETRIEVAL. Retrieval means pulling information out of your long-term memory into the conscious state of short-term memory. Most memory complaints center around people's inability to retrieve information on demand. How many times have you been unable to recall someone's name or a fact during a conversation only to have it "hit" you hours later when you are thinking of something else. The stress of trying to remember something can make the retrieval process difficult, if not impossible. Later, when your mind is more relaxed, you're better able to remember. Another retrieval barrier is lacking a "cue"—a related word, sight, sound or other stimulus—to jog the memory. In other cases, you may have not organized the information well enough when you placed it in long-term memory initially.

There are two ways information can be retrieved from long-term memory: recall and recognition. Recall is a self-initiated search of the long-term memory for information stored previously. Recall is triggered by a cue that you had asso-

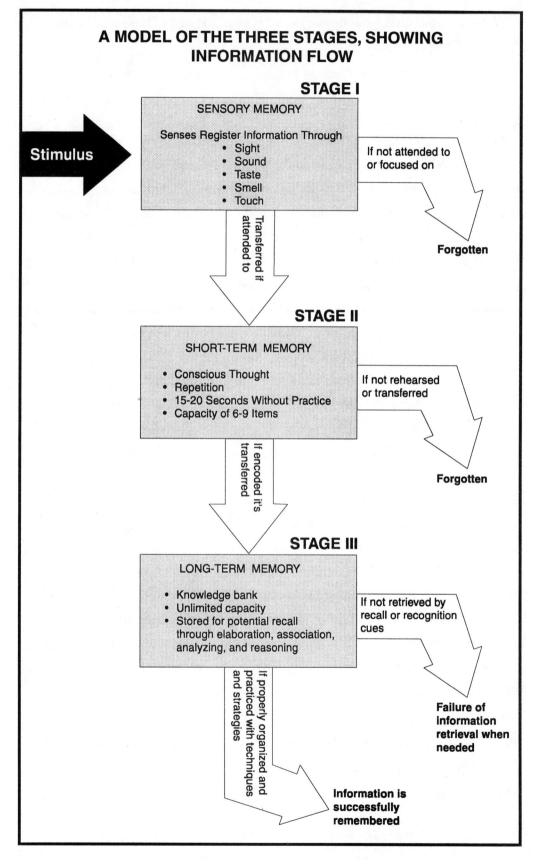

A MODEL OF THE THREE STAGES, SHOWING INFORMATION FLOW

STAGE I

SENSORY MEMORY

Senses Register Information Through
- Sight
- Sound
- Taste
- Smell
- Touch

Stimulus

If not attended to or focused on

Forgotten

Transferred if attended to

STAGE II

SHORT-TERM MEMORY

- Conscious Thought
- Repetition
- 15-20 Seconds Without Practice
- Capacity of 6-9 Items

If not rehearsed or transferred

Forgotten

If encoded it's transferred

STAGE III

LONG-TERM MEMORY

- Knowledge bank
- Unlimited capacity
- Stored for potential recall through elaboration, association, analyzing, and reasoning

If not retrieved by recall or recognition cues

Failure of information retrieval when needed

If properly organized and practiced with techniques and strategies

Information is successfully remembered

ciated with the information. <u>Recognition</u> is perceiving information as something you already know. For most people, recognizing something as familiar is usually easier than recalling something from long-term memory. Unlike recall, which can grow more difficult with age, the ability to recognize is not easily altered by age or circumstances.

Why We Forget

Think of situations that interfere with your ability to recall something from your long-term memory. If you are like most people, you can fall victim to any of a slew of so-called "memory blocks." Memory blocks can often be traced to the way information was originally received or your state of mind when you received it.

EXERCISE 2-1: TROUBLE WITH RECALL

There are many factors that can interfere with memory. Some we can control; others we cannot control. List some factors in the spaces below that tend to interfere with your ability to recall information.

1. _____

2. _____

3. _____

4. _____

5. _____

6. _____

7. _____

8. _____

Compare your responses with those listed below, which have been found to cause most recall failures.

1. <u>Poor listening skills</u>. Not listening carefully enough can prevent you from receiving and retaining what you heard.

2. <u>Physical and psychological stress</u>. Being in emotional or physical pain, for example, can interfere with your ability to learn.

3. <u>Failure to concentrate</u>. You must pay attention to something in order to remember it.

4. <u>Being easily distracted</u>. Extraneous sights and sounds are everywhere. If you let them distract your attention, you could miss remembering something important.

5. <u>Boredom</u>. If you are not interested in what you are hearing or reading, you are less likely to remember it.

6. <u>Too painful or embarrassing</u>. Some memories would cause great emotional upheaval if recalled, so the mind represses them as a self-preservation (defense) mechanism.

7. <u>Fatigue</u>. Sometimes, we are simply too tired to make an effort to store something in our long-term memory.

8. <u>Lack of understanding</u>. If you don't comprehend something, it is difficult or impossible to remember it accurately.

9. <u>Disuse</u>. If the information you are trying to retrieve from your memory is rarely used, it can become difficult or impossible to recall.

10. <u>Learning something similar to what you already know</u>. This can cause you to confuse new information with old information.

11. <u>Absence of a cue</u>. Lacking a word, sight, sound or other sensory stimulus that you associated with a particular memory can make it difficult to locate the information in your knowledge bank.

12. <u>Depression</u>. This will affect your thinking and memory. You will lack any desire or will to remember.

Despite the multitude of reasons for forgetting, it is important to realize that people of all ages occasionally forget and that occasional forgetfulness is normal. Moreover, forgetting isn't necessarily bad. An inability to recall a traumatic incident, for example, can be the mind's way of protecting you from reliving the trauma.

Some things are difficult to remember because you have little or no background knowledge to associate with the new knowledge. Conversely, a memory that successfully entered your knowledge bank may be laden with so much similar information (interference) that it makes the original memory irretrievable. Say you met someone named Jaime Hendrickson last week. This week you were introduced to a James Henderson. The similarities between the two names could cause interference and you may confuse the two names or have trouble remembering one or both.

Another memory problem is caused by information overload. Imagine if you were able to remember every unimportant bit of information that ever entered your short-term memory. Your mind would be crammed with so much trivia that you would have a hard time selecting the useful and relevant items you need to make decisions.

Remembering often takes mental work. Forgetting is far easier.

EXERCISE 2-2: ASSESS YOUR UNDERSTANDING ABOUT FORGETTING

For each of the following statements, write True or False. Answers can be found on the following page.

_____ 1. Forgetting can happen at any age.

_____ 2. Information for which you have few associations and little background knowledge is harder to remember.

_____ 3. If new information is too similar to previously learned information, the original memory can become irretrievable.

_____ 4. There are no valid excuses for not remembering.

_____ 5. Your ability to recall depends on how frequently you retrieve a piece of information and how much time has passed since you last used it.

_____ 6. Forgetting is easier than remembering.

_____ 7. Forgetting is bad.

_____ 8. If you didn't forget, your mind would be cluttered with so much trivia that it would be difficult to recall useful items you need for decision making.

_____ 9. Forgetting unimportant things may help you remember important things.

_____ 10. Forgetting is impossible, even if we try.

Using Observation for Better Concentration

How many times have you wondered whether you remembered to lock your front door or turn off the headlights in your car? These kinds of memory lapses typically occur because you were not paying attention or your attention was divided when doing routine tasks. To overcome these lapses, try to notice some unusual sight, sound, smell, or feeling while doing a routine task. Or think of something bizarre. For example, when you lock your front door, imagine the door laughing hysterically as you turn the key. The more you turn the key, the more the door laughs. This changes a forgettable experience into a memorable one. It also changes your perspective. Instead of simply seeing yourself locking the door, you begin to *observe* yourself locking the door. Just as there is a difference between hearing and listening, there is also a difference between seeing and observing. We can see something, but not observe it. We do it all the time. By using our senses, our imagination, or a combination thereof, we are making a conscious choice to observe something in enough detail to commit it to memory.

Among the most highly trained observers in our culture are law enforcement personnel. Their jobs require them to pay attention to the smallest of details—the color of someone's tie, the texture of a coat, the smell of a room, a license plate number. If bank guards and police officers didn't use all their senses to observe, the outcome could be costly in many ways. You, too, can train yourself to take in details that will help you remember.

EXERCISE 2-3: OBSERVATION PRACTICE

Here are some ways to practice being more observant by consciously using all of your senses.

1. Study a detailed picture in a book or magazine for two minutes. Close the book and list as many details as you can recall from the picture. Look at the picture again. How many details did you remember? How many did you miss? Now try the same exercise with a different picture. Most people are amazed at how many more details they can remember from the second picture.

Continued on next page

Answers to Exercise 2-2: **1,2,3,5,6,8,9 are True; the others are False**

_____

_____

_____

_____

_____

2. Select an object in your home or office that you see every day. Look for something about the object that you never noticed before. For example, there may be a smudge on your toaster, or a small scratch on your steering wheel. This exercise can also work with places or people. If you observe hard enough and use all your senses, it should not be difficult to find features, which had previously been unnoticed, on familiar people, places, and things.

_____

_____

_____

_____

_____

3. List every detail you can think of about your best friend's appearance— facial features, hair color, hair style, skin tone, height, moles, scars, weight, and so on. Next time you see your friend, look at your list? How accurate were your descriptions? What did you miss?

_____

_____

_____

_____

_____

_____

Continued on next page

4. Leave the room you are in. From another location, describe the room you were in with as much detail as possible, including chairs, lamps, wall ornaments, flooring, curtains, blinds, number of windows, location of furniture, and other accessories. Now return to the room to see how well you did.

_____

_____

_____

_____

_____

_____

5. Think of a familiar street and write down everything you can remember about it. Next time you walk down that street, compare your observations with the ones on your list.

_____

_____

_____

_____

_____

6. Without looking at a dollar bill, write down everything you can envision about it. Describe both sides, or try drawing the dollar bill. Now compare your drawing or description with the real thing.

_____

_____

_____

_____

_____

The more you practice the previous exercises, the better your memory will become. In time, being a keen observer will become second nature. This will happen because you have learned to pay attention and concentrate better and take more interest in the world around you.

Learning and Memory

There is no learning without memory.

– Harry Lorayne

To further understand how memory works, it is useful to have a basic understanding of how we learn. Learning is trying to get information into the mind in an understandable and meaningful way. The goal is to retain information in such a way that it can be readily recalled whenever needed.

There are two kinds of learning: intentional and incidental. <u>Intentional</u> learning takes place when you make a conscious effort to learn and remember something new. You have probably already used some memory strategies to learn without being aware of it.

<u>Incidental</u>, or chance, learning occurs whenever you can recall information you had no intention of remembering. Even if you weren't consciously trying to place information in your long-term memory, you must have been paying attention when the information was disseminated.

Different Learning Styles

We all absorb information in three basic ways: visual (seeing), auditory (hearing), and kinesthetic (feeling or doing). Most people prefer one way over the other two. This doesn't mean that we learn through one intake mode at the total exclusion of the other senses. But we all tend to be more successful learning through one of the three modes. Even the words we use can indicate whether we are auditory, visual, or kinesthetic in our learning orientation ("I see what you mean," "I hear you," "I feel your pain").

VISUAL. If you are a visually oriented person, you probably have difficulty absorbing new information through listening or tactile experience. You prefer reading books to listening to books on tape. You may be talented in or otherwise enjoy the visual arts, such as painting or film. For you, "seeing is believing."

AUDITORY. An auditory person likes learning new information by listening to someone talk. You may be clever with words yourself or have a musical ear. Listening is a pleasurable experience for you.

KINESTHETIC. If you are a kinesthetic or tactile person, listening may be a frustrating experience for you. You may also have a poor visual memory. You probably do well in sports and in work that requires motor dexterity, such as sculpture or carpentry. You learn best through personal experience. "Learn by doing" is your motto.

Identifying which learning mode is most successful for you can help improve your memory. Imagine trying to learn to use a piece of new equipment at work. The visual person will probably remember best by seeing a demonstration of how the equipment is operated. An auditory person would prefer listening to someone explain how the machine operates. The kinesthetic person may want to try out the equipment to gain hands-on experience.

Two Hemispheres of the Brain

Although your brain generally functions as a whole, it is divided into two hemispheres. Each hemisphere has specialized functions. The <u>left hemisphere</u> appears to be better at rational thinking, verbal expression, reading, writing, and analytical thinking. Western society tends to value and reward these attributes. Attorneys and accountants are, for the most part, left-brain thinkers.

The <u>right hemisphere</u> deals with spatial ability, artistic appreciation, intuitive thinking, and creative processing. Artists are classic right-brain thinkers.

For each person, one hemisphere is usually more dominant. However, the more connections the hemispheres have with one another at the cellular level, the more powerful the brain is.

In our educational system, the left brain has traditionally received more attention. This is unfortunate because both sides of the brain are equally important to one another. We need to develop both in order to benefit from so-called "whole-brain thinking." Most memory skills are based on visualization and creativity, which are functions of the right brain. In this way, developing better memory skills promotes whole-brain thinking.

Most people assume Albert Einstein was a left-brain thinker because he was a scientist. But Einstein also believed that "imagination is more important than knowledge." His ideas came from visualization. Another classic example of some-

SPECIALIZATIONS OF THE BRAIN

LEFT BRAIN   **RIGHT BRAIN**

The Left Hemisphere

- Logical Thinking
- Analyzing
- Languaging
- Writing
- Reading
- Reasoning
- Mathematics
- Rationalizing
- Sequencing
- Problem solving by breaking down problems
- Remembering names
- Auditory / visual learning

The Right Hemisphere

- Intuitive thinking
- Recognizing faces and patterns
- Creative thinking
- Visualizing images
- Problem solving by looking at the big picture
- Abstract thinking
- Rhythm and musical appreciation
- Imagining / daydreaming
- Parallel processing
- Emotionalizing
- Kinesthetic learning
- Spatially oriented

one who used both brain hemispheres equally was Leonardo da Vinci. He was not only a gifted artist, but also a great scientist, engineer, and architect. He left behind detailed notes depicting very precise analyses of his visual perceptions and concise analytic thinking.

EXERCISE 2-4: LEFT / RIGHT BRAIN SELF-ASSESSMENT

Read the following left and right brain characteristics and circle the statements that describe you most often. The scoring table at the end of the list will help you determine your "dominance." You may find that you are fairly balanced between the two hemispheres.

1. I have no trouble making decisions about the correct thing to do.

2. I see problems or pictures as a whole rather than in parts or details.

3. I follow written directions best and prefer to write and talk.

4. I often think of many things at once rather than thinking through one idea at a time.

5. I'm usually aware of the time.

6. When I'm introduced to someone for the first time, I pay particular attention to the person's face. I later forget the person's name, but I remember his or her face.

7. I attack most problem-solving activities analytically and logically.

8. When comparing things, I usually look for ways they are alike rather than ways they are different.

9. I prefer taking true/false, multiple-choice or matching tests rather than essay tests.

10. Most often, I use my imagination and I think in an abstract manner.

11. If I have a problem, I break it down into smaller, more manageable parts in order to arrive at a solution.

12. I seem to learn best if I can observe a demonstration or read the directions.

13. Generally, I like to be in control of a situation and I do not like to take too many risks.

14. I like assignments that are open-ended rather than more structured assignments.

Continued on next page

15. I learn best by seeing and hearing.

16. I learn best by touching and doing.

17. I usually think in concrete patterns and solve problems with a step-by-step approach.

18. If I try to remember information, I generally picture it in my mind.

19. Although I sometimes get upset, I am a rational person.

20. I don't mind trying anything once; I take risks when it is necessary.

21. Sometimes I talk to myself in order to think or learn something.

22. I can let my feelings "go." I am considered to be somewhat emotional.

23. I solve problems on an intellectual basis rather than an intuitive one.

24. People have told me that I'm creative.

25. I prefer to think of one thing at a time.

26. I like to act in a spontaneous manner.

27. I prefer to plan things and know what's going to happen ahead of time.

28. I can easily remember melodies and tunes.

29. I am usually in control of my feelings.

30. I did well in geometry and geography while in school.

31. I usually can recall information I need quickly and easily.

32. I enjoy reading and writing poetry; it comes to me easily.

33. I can really concentrate when I want to.

34. When I work in a group, I can "feel" the moods of others.

35. I understand mathematical concepts.

36. When solving problems or taking tests, I rely on one idea leading to another in order to come to a conclusion.

37. I can learn new vocabulary words easily.

38. When I plan a party, I "hang loose" rather than plan all of the details.

39. I usually can learn easily from any teacher / trainer.

40. In a classroom setting or a meeting, I'm generally aware of what everyone is doing.

Continued on next page

41. I notice and remember details.

42. I can easily see the whole picture when only a few puzzle pieces are in place.

43. I don't mind practicing something repeatedly in order to master it.

44. I communicate best with someone "in person" rather than on the phone.

45. I can remember jokes and punch lines.

46. I have trouble concentrating when I know I should.

47. I can write directions in a clear and logical manner.

48. I sometimes rely on my intuition when making decisions.

49. I basically have a day-to-day routine.

50. I sometimes can remember things according to where I "saw" them on the page.

SCORING TABLE

_____ Even numbered circled = RIGHT BRAIN ABILITY

_____ Odd numbered circled = LEFT BRAIN ABILITY

Remember, this inventory is only an informal indication of which hemisphere is probably dominant for you. Both sides work together and cannot be totally separated.

SOURCE: Left / Right Brain Self-Assessment adapted from "Learning To Learn" by Gloria Frender, copyright 1990, IP# ISBN 0-86530-141-7, Incentive Publications, Inc., Nashville, TN 37215. Used by permission.

Whole-Brain Learning

To make the most of our mental abilities, society needs to stress "whole brain" learning in the schools and beyond, new research suggests. For example, a pupil studying Abraham Lincoln's Emancipation Proclamation might read texts of his speech, listen to music written by slaves, and perhaps act out a scene from a play written about the era. There is a very strong chance that information imparted through this multi-pronged approach will find its way into the child's long-term memory. Multidisciplinary learning helps build connections between the brain's hemispheres. The hemispheres are complementary because each provides a dimension that the other lacks.

By practicing and applying your powers of observation, concentration, and by using visualization, association, and the memory-enhancing techniques in this book, you can strengthen and develop your right brain as well as your left brain. Creativity occurs when there is a smooth integration between both sides of the brain.

The human mind is more flexible and capable than most people could ever imagine. Whenever you learn something, you literally grow brain tissue. Links between your brain cells via connecting strands called dendrites multiply. The more you are challenged, the more dendrites you grow. Unless there is a specific disease to prevent this from occurring, brain growth can happen throughout life even into old age. This has enormous implications for lifelong learning.

A Mind is a Terrible Thing to Misunderstand

In addition to revelations about the value of whole-brain learning, there are new ideas about the very nature of intelligence. The traditional idea of measuring intelligence with a single IQ number, which puts everyone on a scale ranging from genius to dumb, is falling into disfavor. Instead, researchers say everyone has intelligence, and, in fact, multiple intelligences, but no two people have them in the same combination. Psychologist and writer Howard Gardner says we have at least seven different intelligences:

1. Interpersonal intelligence—the ability to understand other people's moods and concerns.

2. Introspective intelligence—the ability to understand yourself and your own feelings.

3. Spatial intelligence—the knack of visualizing shapes or locations with movement and dimension.

4. Bodily intelligence—when the muscles have their own memory, as with riding a bike.

5. Musical intelligence—the ability to think in sounds in their infinite variety.

6. Verbal intelligence—the ability to use words—spoken, written, or heard.

7. Mathematical or logical intelligence—the ability to understand numbers, symbols, and abstract relationships.

FundaMENTAL #1

Improve Your Self-concept

Gardner asserts that instead of asking, "How smart are you?", intelligence tests should ask, "How are you smart?" Discovering what you are good at is critical to success; the more you use your natural talents, the happier you will be. We must recognize each person's unique intelligence, Gardner emphasizes in his books and television appearances.

FundaMENTAL #1: Improve Your Self-concept

The fate of your memory is not chance but choice.

– Phil Bruschi

Your attitude determines your altitude when it comes to work, relationships, and everything else in life—including your memory. You need to come to grips with the kind of person you are when it comes to lifelong learning. Some older people continue to develop their intellectual ability throughout their lives. These people would never use aging as an excuse for not learning. Others are not highly motivated to discover new things or challenge themselves. They may claim they are too old to learn anything new. Which end of this spectrum are you closest to? The following exercise aims to help you find out.

EXERCISE 2-5: IDENTIFYING YOUR MEMORY EXPECTATIONS

What is your attitude toward continued learning? Are your expectations about your learning potential generally negative or positive? Your responses to the following questions should help crystallize your expectations.

What have you done recently that contributed to your mental growth (e.g., took a class, taught a class, attended a play, read a book)?

_____

_____

_____

What is stopping you from learning new things (e.g., lack of energy, lack of time, lack of interest)?

_____

_____

_____

EXERCISE 2-6: NEGATIVE EXPECTATIONS AND MEMORY POISON

Check any of the following statements that are familiar to you.

_____ "I'm terrible when it comes to remembering names."

_____ "My memory is getting worse with age."

_____ "I'm not interested in trying to remember; I'm retired now."

_____ "I'll never be able to learn this computer program."

_____ "What's the use in learning anything new; I can't remember it anyway."

_____ "I can't understand this information, so why even try."

_____ "I'm too old to learn anything new."

_____ "I hope I don't have to take a test; I usually freeze up and forget everything."

_____ "I just know I'm going to forget my speech when I'm in front of all those people."

_____ "Please remind me to pick that up on my way home or I'll forget."

Can you add any others?

_____

_____

_____

_____

_____

_____

These types of statements can produce a negative self-concept, which poison your expectations. If you expect to fail, you are likely to put minimal effort into remembering important information, and you might actually avoid tasks that require you to remember.

Additionally, a negative self-concept can lead to anxiety and stress. Inner distress is usually accompanied by fear and physical symptoms. For example, some people become sick to their stomach at the thought of making a speech because they are afraid of forgetting and embarrassing themselves. Fear is very common in people who tend to view themselves in a negative light. Often, these fears are irrational. Fear and anxiety reduce your ability to focus and pay attention. That often leads to memory failure.

If you exhibit one or more of the following symptoms for more than a brief period, you may be suffering from chronic anxiety and stress, which could explain some of your memory problems. (These symptoms may also indicate medical problems, so see your doctor.)

- ❑ Inability to concentrate
- ❑ Sleeplessness
- ❑ Panic attacks
- ❑ Constant worrying
- ❑ Heart palpitations
- ❑ Increase in body temperature
- ❑ Light-headedness
- ❑ Fear of physical illness
- ❑ Inability to relax
- ❑ Excessive perspiring

EXERCISE 2-7: POSITIVE EXPECTATIONS—ANTIDOTE FOR THE POISON

Becoming aware of your self-defeating thoughts and their destructive potential is the first step toward self-improvement. The second step is turning those negative thoughts around in order to boost your expectations. Next time you think of one of those negative phrases, replace it with one of the following positive affirmations, or come up with some of your own.

"I'm not certain this will work, but I'll give it a try."

"I'm nervous about giving this presentation, but it will be an opportunity for growth and development."

"I can get better at remembering names if I try harder."

Continued on next page

"I know older people who have a terrific memory."

"It may take time to learn this material, but I am capable of understanding it."

Add more positive statements here:

_____

_____

_____

_____

_____

By using positive affirmations as often as possible, you will reduce the stress associated with self-deprecation. Here are some other ways to relieve stress and anxiety while improving your self-concept:

- *Don't let yourself get overloaded with too much information at once.* In this information age, this is easy to do. When doing research, for example, keep your scope narrow enough to conquer without undue difficulty. If your subject matter is extensive, break it down into smaller components and tackle them one at a time. Pace yourself. Try not to remember everything all at once.

- *Talk to your physician.* Doctors, particularly osteopaths and others who take a holistic approach to medicine, may have some suggestions on how to reduce the stress in your life.

- *Consider biofeedback.* Biofeedback shows the connection between your mental and physical states and can literally train your mind and body to relax.

- *Try not to worry about things that you cannot control.* You can't solve everybody's problems.

- *Face your fears.* For example, if you have the option of making an oral presentation at work, take the risk even if you've always been afraid of public speaking. At the very least, the experience will give you a chance to practice your new memory skills.

- *Don't let the idea of getting old get you down.* Many cultures revere their elders. Let your wrinkles and gray hair symbolize wisdom and survival instead of the loss of youth.

- *Work harder at staying fit and healthy.* The physical and psychological benefits of regular aerobic exercise cannot be overemphasized.

- *Practice the memory strategies offered later in Parts Two and Three of this book.* Use the strategies every chance you get.

- *Get organized.* Lack of organization at home or work can waste time, produce anxiety, and interfere with memory.

- *Seek out help whenever you need it.* Ask friends and coworkers what works for them when they need to remember something. Or read books like this one, or listen to an audio program on memory improvement. (Several are listed in the bibliography at the end of this book.)

- *Don't make unrealistic demands on your memory.* Setting goals is fine, but make sure your goals are realistic and attainable. When learning new information, you may need to give yourself more time to study. This is especially true as we get older. Concentration becomes more difficult with age because we tend to be more easily distracted. With the myth about aging and senility so pervasive in our society, a negative self-concept can be reinforced every time an older person makes a mistake or forgets something. Just because you mislaid your glasses doesn't mean you have Alzheimer's disease. No one's memory is fail-proof.

- *Notice and celebrate the many memory successes you have every day.* It is easy to take these things for granted.

- *Allow yourself the freedom to forget.* Understand that it is all right not to remember everything.

- *Be more selective about what you need to remember, and disregard what you don't need.* You do this by deciding what to pay attention to and what to ignore.

- *Don't give up.* A lack of self-confidence about your memory can result in half-hearted memory efforts. Giving up on a memory task when you could be successful is the easy way out. Sometimes a little persistence makes all the difference.

If your attitude toward memory enhancement is negative, you probably won't do much learning, problem solving, or creative thinking. Perhaps you are stymied by a fear of failure. This fear may stem from the mistaken belief that the brain is supposed to deteriorate as one ages. If you avoid challenges or have someone else do your problem-solving for you, you will miss opportunities to exercise your mind. By failing to stimulate your brain cells, you risk setting yourself up for memory difficulties.

MEMORY AND AGING

Although researchers have identified some memory changes that are associated with normal aging, the large majority of older people will not experience severe memory loss. People's memory skills and capacity to remember vary widely. Because of this individual variation, aging affects everyone's memory differently. Although most people believe memory declines with age, older people generally experience memory reduction only in certain areas. For instance, as people get older, glitches tend to occur more often in short-term memory. Long-term memory appears to remain intact. Health problems and low self-esteem, both of which can impede memory, are more prevalent among older people. Specifically, diseases such as Alzheimer's, Parkinson's, Picks, and Huntington's all impair memory function to varying degrees.

Normal changes associated with aging include:

- *Difficulty paying attention.* Distractions and interruptions can become more difficult to ignore, which often makes us forget more easily. Seniors should be proactive in this area. If you can't concentrate on a conversation because of disturbing background noise, for example, move to a quieter room, or turn down the music. Senior citizens often must make a conscious effort to relax, use all their senses to acquire new information, and jot things down more frequently.

- *Slower thinking.* All of our systems become less efficient as we age, including our thinking, memory, and problem-solving abilities. You may need to review new information several times in order to learn it.

- *Slower recall.* As we age, our ability to retrieve information from long-term memory slows down. Older people have acquired a lifetime worth of facts in their memory; it is not surprising that retrieving information takes longer. Don't let that discourage you.

- *Less frequent use of memory strategies.* Older adults are less likely to use strategies such as association, imagination, visualization, and organization. More research is needed to determine whether they do not consciously use these strategies or whether they do not apply them efficiently. Motivation also plays a key role in the use of such techniques.

- *Need for more memory cues.* As we age, we need more cues more often in order to recall information. As you may recall, memory cues are bits of related information that help us remember a specific item. For example, if you are trying to remember the name of your cousin's new husband, you may think of your cousin, visualize her husband's face, think of where he works, and your most recent conversation with him. All these cues can help you locate his name in your memory.

- *Depression.* Losing a spouse or friend, retiring, or moving can produce stress and depression, which can reduce your ability to concentrate and remember.

- *Sensory impairment.* Some older people suffer vision or hearing impairment, which impedes their ability to receive information. Certain medications and drug interactions also can affect mood and memory. If you suspect this may be happening to you, report your concerns to your doctor or pharmacist. Chronic alcoholism also can lead to serious memory impairment.

The news isn't all bad. Senior citizens are generally wiser, have a broader vocabulary, are more sensitive to others, and are better at judging and evaluating new information. These attributes can be used to meet some of the new memory challenges that face us all during our golden years.

MEMORY ENHANCEMENT TECHNIQUES FOR THE LATER YEARS

The following strategies are designed to improve your memory. These strategies can be effective at any age.

1. Focus your mind on the information to be remembered.

2. Remove distractions—or remove yourself from a distracting environment—whenever possible.

3. Believe in your natural ability to remember.

4. Give yourself sufficient time to learn something you want to remember. Ask people to speak a little slower or louder, if necessary.

5. As often as you can, reminisce with a friend or family member. It will help you remember names and events.

6. Create a "memory place" in your office and home where you always put your keys, glasses, watch, wallet, or other important items.

7. Use your imagination to associate names with faces when you meet someone new.

8. Group things into categories that are easy to remember. For example, if you are leaving on a trip and you need to remember five unrelated things, group them under such categories as <u>house</u> (lock it, turn on lights), <u>documents</u> (passport, airline tickets), <u>pets</u> (take dog to kennel, give neighbor key to feed cat).

9. Make a "To Do" list, and post it prominently.

10. Don't panic if you forget something. Otherwise you may fall into the trap of thinking that every minor memory lapse is a sign of senility.

EXERCISE 2-8: STEPS TO IMPROVE YOUR MEMORY CONFIDENCE

In the space below, list steps you can take to improve your self-confidence about your memory (e.g., Write a "to-do" list and prioritize it at the end of each workday to help organize the next day's responsibilities).

1. _____

2. _____

3. _____

4. _____

5. _____

The gray matters, so stay in shape!

FundaMENTAL #2

Increase Your Powers of Attention and Concentration

FundaMENTAL #2: Increase Your Powers of Attention and Concentration

An object once attended to will remain in memory,
whereas one inattentively allowed to pass, will leave no trace.

– William James

Increasing your powers of attention and concentration is the second funda-MENTAL that can release your memory power. If you are not paying attention to the subject at hand, you are not listening. Listening for better recall is often overlooked but essential for retaining information. "Information must be strongly registered" in order to be remembered, states memory expert and author Stuart Reid. Attention deficits account for about half of all reported memory problems, according to another memory expert, Danielle Lapp.

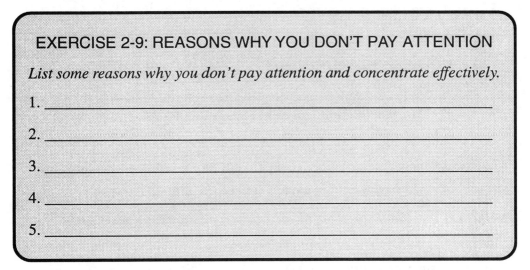

EXERCISE 2-9: REASONS WHY YOU DON'T PAY ATTENTION

List some reasons why you don't pay attention and concentrate effectively.

1. _____

2. _____

3. _____

4. _____

5. _____

Having studied and taught memory-enhancement skills for two decades, I have discovered a variety of reasons why people fail to pay attention and concentrate. The following is a list of the most common ones. How many apply to you?

1. *Listening skills were never specifically taught in school.* Emphasis has been placed on teaching other communications skills, such as reading, writing, and speaking.

2. *We can't cope with information overload.* As a result, there is trouble discerning important from unimportant information. Lack of coping skills produces stress and anxiety, which is often associated with information overload.

3. *We let our mind wander when we should be concentrating.* The brain is capable of comprehending anywhere from 600 to 800 words per minute when someone is speaking. Since the average person speaks only 100 to 140 words per minute, it is easy to think about something else with all that "leftover" time. For most of us, training our mind to maintain focus when someone is talking takes discipline and practice.

4. *We buy into the myth that talking represents power, and that listening is somehow subservient.* So, in conversations, we impatiently wait for someone to stop talking so we can speak.

5. *We hear only what we want to hear.* To some extent, virtually everyone filters information through personal biases, sometimes to their own detriment.

6. *Physical factors such as hearing impairment or fatigue make it difficult to listen.*

7. *Our biases, opinions, and prejudices can dissuade us from paying attention to people we disagree with.*

8. *We allow environmental influences such as noise, visual stimuli, interruptions, and even room temperature to distract us.*

9. *Lack of interest or motivation.* If we are not interested in something, we don't bother to pay attention, even if the information is important.

10. *Allowing bad habits, such as daydreaming and interrupting, to prevail.*

11. *We have no clear purpose or plan in mind.* Lacking an objective for paying attention, such as an upcoming exam, it can be difficult to stay focused.

12. *Preoccupation with our emotional state or other concerns.*

IMPROVING ATTENTION SKILLS: WHAT'S IN IT FOR ME?

Beyond improving memory, learning to pay attention and concentrate more effectively yields other important benefits. You can:

1. Save time, money, effort, and in some cases, lives. (Listening effectively on the job, for example, can help you avoid costly errors.)

2. Avoid embarrassment.

3. Increase your confidence.

4. Have more peace of mind.

5. Accomplish more goals.

6. Improve your understanding.

7. Control distractions more easily.

8. Ask better questions.

9. Be more valued and trusted by your boss and coworkers.

10. Build better personal and professional relationships.

ATTENTION AND CONCENTRATION BEHAVIORS AND ATTITUDES

Building attention skills is an ongoing process, one that you must commit to every day in your listening situations. It is the only way to meet your memory challenges head-on. Noticing your listening behaviors and changing ones that need changing will improve your memory. To discover your personal attitudes and behaviors, complete the following exercise.

EXERCISE 2-10: ATTENTION/CONCENTRATION SELF-ASSESSMENT

Answer Yes (Y) or No (N) to each of the following statements as it describes your attitude or behavior most of the time.

( ) I get distracted easily.

( ) I ask questions whenever I don't understand something.

( ) I try not to interrupt people when they are talking.

( ) I maintain good eye contact when I am speaking with someone.

( ) My mind jumps ahead when listening to a speaker.

( ) I allow someone to finish what they are saying before forming opinions.

( ) I use my body language to show that I am interested in what someone is saying to me.

( ) I don't fake paying attention.

Continued on next page

( ) I'm always thinking of my responses when listening to a speaker.

( ) I restate or paraphrase what the speaker just said to make sure I understand.

( ) I am patient when listening to others.

( ) I take effective notes.

( ) I'm aware of my biases and try to control them when listening.

( ) I'm careful not to let my emotions get in the way of listening.

( ) I don't focus my attention on more than one thing at a time.

( ) I try to put the speaker's needs above my own.

( ) I tend to daydream when

( ) I don't look for excuses for

( ) I show the speaker that I am attentive by using non-verbal postures and gestures.

( ) I try to maintain eye contact when someone is talking to me.

( ) Whenever possible, I control my environment so it is free from distractions when I am trying to learn.

KEY

1-5 "No" responses = Excellent attention and concentration skills

6-10 "No" responses = Good, but there is room for improvement

11-15 "No" responses = You need more practice paying attention and concentrating

16-20 "No" responses = Your lack of good attention and concentration skills is putting you at risk for memory trouble. But, don't worry—*MIND AEROBICS* can help. Feel free to take this test again after practicing the memory techniques described in this book.

20 STRATEGIES TO IMPROVE YOUR ATTENTION AND CONCENTRATION

In order to improve your memory, you must become an "active listener"—that is someone who can concentrate and pay attention effectively. Doing this requires making a commitment to practice one or more of the strategies described below. Select those strategies that feel most natural to you. The more strategies you can master, the easier it will be to become an active listener.

1. *"Set" your mind to listen.* Before entering a meeting or lecture hall, for example, make a conscious decision that you will pay attention and concentrate throughout the session. If your mind starts to wander, redirect your attention immediately.

2. *Ignore distractions, be they internal or external.* That means not worrying about what you will have for dinner in the middle of listening to a sales presentation. That also means ignoring an annoying whisper two rows behind you during a training seminar.

3. *Anticipate.* Trying to guess (internally) what a speaker will say next may help keep your attention focused.

4. *Pay attention to a speaker's cues,* such as his or her voice, gestures, rate of speech, posture, facial expressions, volume, etc. All help clarify the speaker's message.

5. *From time to time, ask yourself what the speaker's main points are.*

6. *Give special attention to any information that is repeated.* If a speaker's point is important enough to be repeated, it is probably worth learning and committing to long-term memory.

7. *Periodically sum up the speaker's main points in your head.* This will help prevent your mind from wandering.

8. *Listen with your whole body,* including your ears, mind, heart, eyes, and posture. Totally absorbing yourself in this way helps satisfy the speaker's need to be listened to, as well as your need to learn and remember.

9. *Take notes.* The very act of writing things down helps you visualize what you need to remember and develops your motor skill memory. Your notes will also help you review information later on. (Note taking should be used as an adjunct to, not a replacement for, other listening and memory techniques.)

10. *Plan to report the information to someone else later.* Knowing you'll need to relay the information to a third party gives you a reason to pay attention even if you are not personally interested in what is being said.

11. *Develop an opportunistic attitude.* Even if the main theme of what you are listening to is of little interest, there may be morsels of information here and there that you can use. Listening for those morsels will improve your concentration.

12. *Seek out complex information.* Trying to understand difficult concepts will "exercise" your mind and force you to concentrate better.

13. *Listen actively, not passively.* Give the speaker feedback on what he or she just said. Don't pretend you are paying attention when you're not.

14. *Use your imagination to form mental images of the information you are receiving.* This forces you to use the left and right sides of your brain simultaneously.

15. *Take advantage of the time lapse between how fast a person is talking and how much faster your mind can absorb information.* Use the extra time to ask yourself questions about what is being said, summarize the material, or anticipate what the speaker will say next.

16. *Take frequent breaks—every 30 to 60 minutes, if possible—so you can get refreshed and re-energized.* Breaks also give your brain time to integrate the information it has just received.

17. *Maintain good health.* Your ability to pay attention is closely linked to your physical health; a healthy body equals a healthy mind. Keep fit through good nutrition and regular exercise.

18. *Be observant.* Take in as many details of a situation as possible. This will help you remember an experience more fully.

19. *Try to control your emotions.* Strong emotional responses can lead you to tune out information you need to learn or cause you to skew it before placing it in your long-term memory.

20. *Practice, practice, practice.* Every day brings new opportunities to practice your attention and concentration skills. Continual practice will produce noticeable improvements in your memory.

MEMORY CHECK

In the space below, write down the most important points you learned from Part Two.

_____

_____

_____

_____

_____

_____

_____

_____

_____

_____

_____

_____

_____

_____

_____

_____

_____

_____

_____

_____

_____

_____

FundaMENTAL #3

Keep Your Mind Active

PART THREE

TRAINING YOUR MEMORY

Now that you know how memory works and how to improve your natural memory, you are ready for advanced guidelines to boost your memory skills. Let's begin with the next fundaMENTAL.

FundaMENTAL #3: Keep Your Mind Active

What causes brain cells to weaken is decreased workload, blood supply, and lack of stimulation.

— **Tony Robbins**

The best way to keep your mind active, and thereby increase your memory power, is to expose yourself to rich, varied, and stimulating experiences as often as possible. Here are a few suggestions:

- Take classes on subjects you have always been interested in.

- Learn a new skill you can use for work, school, or recreation.

- Join social clubs or professional associations where you can meet new people.

- Read as much as you can. Detective and mystery books, in particular, exercise your memory and powers of observation.

- Watch educational or how-to television shows that really make you think. Examples include PBS specials, Discovery Channel biographies, "This Old House," or "Home Time" that show you how to install plumbing, build a deck, or do other home improvements.

- Travel. Seeing new places, even if they are close to home, can be enormously stimulating.

- Get involved in community work.

- Teach or consult, if you have an expertise that can help others.

- Engage in a new, stimulating hobby, such as painting, sculpting, or getting involved in community theater.

- Become involved politically. If there is a local or national issue you care about, learn as much as you can and find ways to educate others.

Engaging in mental exercises is another way of keeping your mind active. Many folks work hard at keeping their bodies in shape but do little to keep their minds fit. Too many people don't realize that the mind can be developed and conditioned through a program of mental exercise. The key is incorporating mental exercises into your daily life.

MIND AEROBICS is a system of mental conditioning designed to improve memory function. Problem solving is to the brain what aerobic exercise is to the body. It's one of the best ways to keep your brain in peak condition. By exercising your mind, you can optimize your memory. Studies have shown that the key to avoiding mental aging is keeping your mind active. Whenever you concentrate on something, new connections form between brain cells. This makes the brain more powerful.

In his "Living Health" seminar, world renowned author and speaker Tony Robbins talks about the importance of keeping brain cells active. He believes that brain cells weaken when their work load is decreased, their blood supply diminished, and when they lack stimulation. The simple act of learning constitutes mental exercise. The human mind is more flexible and capable than most people imagine. The very act of learning new information is part of my *MIND AEROBICS* approach. If your job is not giving you the opportunity for challenge, stimulation, or problem solving, have a talk with your supervisor about new learning opportunities.

Here, then, are some exercises and suggestions designed to give you a mental workout. The only equipment you need is a pencil, paper, and your mind.

WARM-UP MENTAL EXERCISES

The following exercises are designed to stretch your mind soon after waking up. You can do these exercises in bed, in the shower, or at breakfast. Do each step as fast as possible. Speak out loud or to yourself.

Step 1:	Count backwards from 50 to 1
Step 2:	Name 20 friends or relatives (first names only)
Step 3:	Name 15 fruits and vegetables
Step 4:	Name 20 states or cities

Do these warm-up exercises daily for two or three weeks as soon as possible after you wake up. If you get distracted, don't start over; just pick up where you left off. Here is where good concentration skills come into play. Don't worry about getting all the answers right. It's the process that matters most.

SHORT-TERM MEMORY EXERCISE #1

Study the list below for 20 seconds. Then close the book and recall as many items from the list as you can over the next 60 seconds. Don't worry about the order. Just write down as many items as you can remember.

Bus	**Cowboy hat**	**Dog**
Saw	**Shoes**	**Pipe**
Chair	**Horse**	**Ladder**
Ruler	**Spoon**	**Book**
Baseball glove	**Clock**	**Eagle**

SCORING
   10 or more items in less than 1 minute – Excellent
   10 or more items in 1 minute – Very Good
   7 to 9 items in less than 1 minute – Good
   7 to 9 items in 1 minute – Fair

SHORT-TERM MEMORY EXERCISE # 2

Closely observe the numbers and shapes below for one minute. Close the book, and time yourself as you write down which numbers are in squares, circles, triangles, and rectangles.

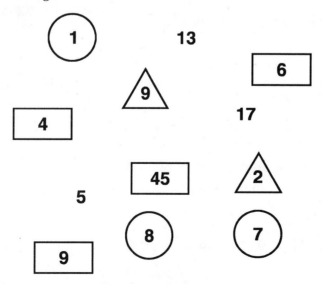

SCORING
3 right in under 1 minute – Excellent
3 right in 1 minute – Very Good
3 right in under 75 seconds – Good
3 right in 75 seconds – Fair

SHORT-TERM MEMORY EXERCISE #3

Closely observe the letters below for 20 seconds. Close the book and time how long it takes you to write the word that can be formed using all the letters. (The answer can be found at the bottom of page 52.)

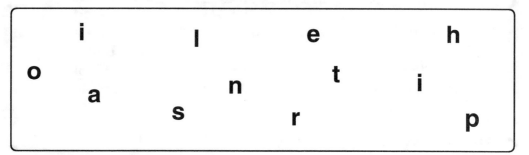

SCORING
If you figure out the word in . . .
5 seconds – Excellent
10 seconds – Very Good
15 seconds – Good
20 to 30 seconds – Fair

SHORT-TERM MEMORY EXERCISE #4

Study the following sets of numbers for 35 seconds. Close the book and write both sets as fast as you can. Sequence is not important.

SCORING
If you get the answer in less than 45 seconds – Excellent
If you get the answer in 45 seconds – Very Good
If you get the answer in less than 1 minute – Good
If you get the answer in 1 minute – Fair

SHORT-TERM MEMORY EXERCISE #5

Study the drawing below for 15 seconds. Close the book and try to replicate the drawing on a blank piece of paper as fast as you can.

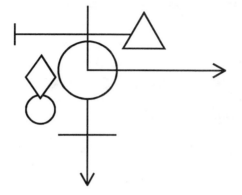

SCORING

If you can complete the drawing in . . .

15 seconds or less – Excellent
15-30 seconds – Very Good
31-44 seconds – Good
45 seconds – Fair

SHORT-TERM MEMORY EXERCISE #6

Closely observe the map below for three minutes. Close the book and in less than one minute, replicate the map on a blank piece of paper including as many features as possible, such as street names, places, things, etc.

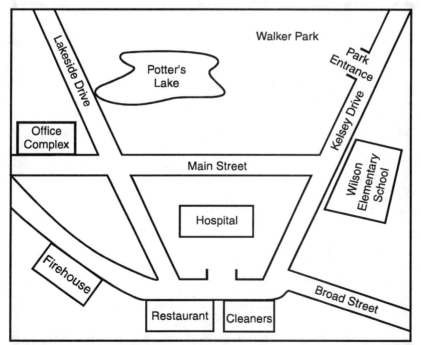

SCORING

10 or more features in under 1 minute – Excellent

10 or more features in 1 minute – Very Good

7 to 9 features in under 1 minute – Good

7 to 9 features in 1 minute – Fair

SHORT-TERM MEMORY EXERCISE #7

Read the directions below slowly.

You are traveling down Highway 41 for exactly 12 miles when you come to an intersection where there is a gas station on one corner and a car dealership on the other. You make a left onto Route 538 and drive another 15 minutes until you pass through a small town called Spotswood. Go to the third traffic light and make a right turn. Look for the town's municipal building on your left. Make a left onto Brookdale Road. Go two blocks, and make a left onto Chelsea Drive. The house is a white, two-story colonial, number 437.

Without looking at the directions you just read, answer the following questions as fast as you can.

1. How many miles did you travel on Highway 41?_____

2. What was at the intersection of Highway 41 and Route 538? _____

_____

3. What was the name of the small town? _____

4. How many blocks do you pass on Brookdale Road before turning left on Chelsea Drive? _____

SCORING

4 right answers in 15 seconds – Excellent

3 right answers in 15 seconds – Good

2 right answers in 15 seconds – Fair

Answer to Exercise #3: Relationship

Remember to train your brain,
because no brain, no gain!

FundaMENTAL #4

Use Visualization, Association, and Imagination

Remember, the point of all these exercises is to keep your mind as active as possible, which slows down mental aging. Look for other problem-solving exercises on your own (e.g., brain teasers, riddles, crossword puzzles) to give your brain a mental workout. By challenging your mind, your memory will improve. Next, you will see how you can use visualization and association techniques to help you remember.

FundaMENTAL #4: Use Visualization, Association, and Imagination

If we would allow ourselves to become like a child again and see things through a child's eyes, mind, and body, we could learn anything.

– David Meir

Another fundaMENTAL of memory fitness is <u>visualization</u>. Because much of the information stored in our long-term memory is visual, using images when committing things to memory is an effective tool. The concept of mental imagery is used frequently in the field of psychology, among other things, to help people obtain their goals. Positive imagery is used in sports psychology, psychotherapy, and other areas where people are working to achieve success.

Simply put, visualization is your mind's ability to picture an event or item. The ability to create clear, vivid mental images varies among individuals, with a small fraction of the population claiming they can't generate mental images at all. I believe that every person can learn to use his/her imagination to visualize. Aristotle said: "A vivid imagination compels the whole body to obey it." And Oliver Wendel Holmes, the Supreme Court Justice, said, "You don't quit playing because you grow old; you grow old because you quit playing." Children use imaginative play all the time. Unfortunately, as adults, we tend to think that imagination is something we have outgrown.

Today, many companies and organizations seek out imaginative people to find creative solutions to problems. Creativity is a lifelong process, and there is no reason adults can't learn to think more creatively and vividly. Visual images transcend language barriers and communicate quickly and effectively. Consider the influx of road signs that now use pictures instead of words.

By increasing your ability to picture things in your mind's eye, your memory will improve automatically. Visual images are some of the most useful memory joggers. You will find them extremely helpful in using the memory aids and techniques that follow. Memory aids are also known as <u>mnemonics</u>. Mnemonics are named after Mnemosyne, the Greek goddess of memory. Mnemonics exercise your mind in two ways. One, they force you to concentrate by associating new information with information you already know and visualizing what you are trying to learn. Two, mnemonics will strengthen your short-term memory by using your imagination to create illogical pictures. Ridiculous, nonsensical, bizarre, or hilarious mental images tend to stick in your memory because they stand out from the logical things we think about all day.

To demonstrate this concept, form a mental picture in your mind's eye of a hippopotamus sitting on top of a flagpole—or something else outside the realm of possibility. It's possible to imagine all kinds of crazy scenes by thinking about them, and with practice, you can get good at it. The next challenge is connecting or associating your illogical mental pictures to things you want to remember. This is a powerful way to lock important information into your long-term memory.

VISUALIZATION TIPS

Illogical mental pictures can play in your mind like a cartoon. Cartoons are very illogical, and cartoonists are some of our culture's most imaginative people. Here are several tips that can help you create cartoon-like images in your mind.

1. Visualize objects far smaller or far bigger than they actually are.

2. Visualize objects in action.

3. Exaggerate the number of objects—hundreds or thousands.

4. Visualize in color.

5. Use your imagination to turn an object into something else that sounds or looks like the original object but is more meaningful to you.

6. Put yourself or someone else into the picture.

7. Visualize the object in a scene that can't possibly happen in real life.

8. Include emotions in your mental pictures; try to feel the emotions.

9. Visualize in as much detail as possible.

10. Imagine objects using all your senses.

The above tips work best for concrete objects or action scenes. Abstract concepts—such as loyalty, honor, guilt, and admiration—are far more difficult to "see" in your mind's eye.

ASSOCIATION

Be it trained or untrained, everyone's memory is based on <u>association</u>. Memory relies on an organized system of associating new information with previously learned information. The best way to remember information is to associate it with something you already know. So, the process of association uses visualization.

Asking questions is one way we use association. When you hear a new idea you wish to remember, ask yourself the following: Why is this idea worth remembering? When might the idea be useful? How might I use this idea? Where might I use this idea? Where did this idea come from? Answering these questions will help you form a complete picture of the idea and help you remember it. You will find that when issues are supported by answers to these key questions, they will stay in your memory. By asking and answering these questions, you are bringing association from the subconscious realm to the conscious realm where it can be deliberately used as a memory-enhancing device.

LINKING. <u>Linking</u>, also known as <u>chaining</u>, is a mnemonic aid that uses visualization to associate any number of items or ideas in sequential order. These items or ideas are linked together to form a chain. It helps to think of linking as a game.

The first rule of the game is to think of an absurd picture to associate two items. In forming links of a memory chain, one item must lead you to the next item if you are to remember correctly. The exercise below will give you an opportunity to develop and practice your linking skills in a story format. Use all your senses to visualize, associate, and imagine the story in your mind.

EXERCISE 3-2: THE PLANETS-PART A

List the planets of our solar system according to their distance from the sun (from closest to farthest). (The answers can be found at the bottom of page 60.)

1. _____

2. _____

3. _____

4. _____

5. _____

6. _____

7. _____

8. _____

9. _____

In case you didn't do too well, here's a way to learn the planets in order using the linking system format. This format helps you learn faster and is more fun than rote memorization. As you read the illogical story that follows, try to envision how each part is linked to the next. Remember, use all of your senses as you visualize each scene—smell the odors, hear the sounds, see everything in vivid detail. Read through the story two or three times to get it into your long-term memory. Note that many of the visualization tips already discussed are used in the story. Remember to concentrate and stay focused as you read.

THE PLANETS-PART B: A CELESTIAL STORY

It is a bright, sunny day, and you are standing in a beautiful meadow. Feel the sun's warmth on your face. Smell the sweet fragrance of the flowers. Hear the birds chirping. Feel the tall green grass beneath your feet. You are very relaxed and calm. Suddenly, a shiny, red 1955 <u>Mercury</u> pulls up and stops about five feet in front of you. As you stand there startled, the ground begins to shake as if a giant were walking nearby. You turn around to see a 15-foot-tall goddess. It's <u>Venus</u>. You notice how beautiful she is as she smiles down at you. Across the meadow in a wooded area you hear a strange singing voice, and <u>Eartha</u> Kitt comes out of a woods carrying a <u>Mars</u> bar in her hand. She climbs into the back seat of the car and devours the candy. At that moment, the sky opens up with crashing thunder and lightning, and who should appear on the roof of the car but <u>Jupiter</u>, the Roman god of the heavens. Jupiter points with his scepter to a gold, blazing license plate on the front bumper which reads "SUN," an acronym for <u>Saturn</u>, <u>Uranus</u>, and <u>Neptune</u>. As the car speeds out of the meadow, <u>Pluto</u>, god of the Underworld, hurls a ball of fire at the car as it speeds out of sight.

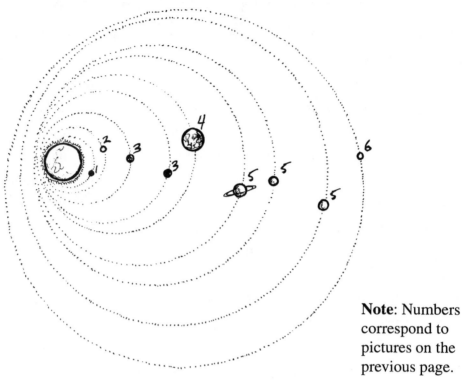

Note: Numbers correspond to pictures on the previous page.

Without referring to the story, list the nine planets from memory. If you had visualized how each part of the story was linked to the next, you should have no trouble naming all the planets now, in the right order.

PEGGING. Pegging is one of the most effective memory strategies that uses association. As with linking, you'll need your powers of visualization and imagination to use the peg system. Basically, pegging involves associating numbers to mental images. Numbers are abstract, so meaning must be given to each number by way of association. By "hanging" new items to be remembered on established, or "pegged," images, you can remember virtually any list—backward, forward, in or out of sequence. In a sense, pegging establishes a permanent storage place in your memory where new information can be engraved.

The first step is to create a peg list by associating a specific mental image to a number. As you will see, this can be done in a variety of ways, including logical associations. It may not seem apparent at first, but the following sample peg list is based on logical associations and mental pictures.

Answers to Exercise 3-2: 1. Mercury, 2. Venus, 3. Earth, 4. Mars, 5. Jupiter, 6. Saturn, 7. Uranus, 8. Neptune, 9. Pluto

---

PEGGING EXERCISE #1: LOGIC PEG LIST

Study the list below for three minutes in the numerical order they appear. Then turn the page.

1. Pencil

2. Faucet

3. Triangle

4. Table

5. Fingers

6. Beer

7. Dice

8. Skate

9. Cat

10. Indians

11. Ladder

12. Bread Rolls

13. Ghosts

14. Gold Ring

15. Tax Form

16. Candles

17. Car

18. Flag

19. Golf Shoes

20. Money

Now, write as many items as you can remember next to its corresponding number below. When you are finished, look at the previous page to see how well you've done.

1. _____ 11. _____

2. _____ 12. _____

3. _____ 13. _____

4. _____ 14. _____

5. _____ 15. _____

6. _____ 16. _____

7. _____ 17. _____

8. _____ 18. _____

9. _____ 19. _____

10. _____ 20. _____

Here is the logic that was used to select the items for each number:

Number	Word	Logical Association
1	Pencil	Number "1" looks like a pencil
2	Faucet	"2" positions: hot & cold or on & off; faucet is a "2"-syllable word
3	Triangle	"3" sides, corners, or angles
4	Table	"4" legs on a table
5	Fingers	"5" fingers on a hand
6	Beer	"6" pack of beer
7	Dice	Lucky "7"
8	Skate	Rhymes with "8" or figure "8"
9	Cat	"9" lives
10	Indians	"10" Little Indians song
11	Ladder	"11" looks like the sides of a ladder
12	Bread Rolls	A dozen bread rolls
13	Ghosts	"13" is a superstitious number. You are superstitious if you believe in ghosts.

Number	Word	Logical Association
14	Gold Ring	"14"-karat gold ring
15	Taxes	April "15" income tax deadline
16	Candles	"16" candles (song)/sweet "16"
17	Car	"17" legal age to drive in most states
18	Flag	"18" is age to vote, flag at polling location
19	Golf Shoes	Take off shoes and relax at "19th" hole for refreshments
20	Money	"20" rhymes with "money"

There are other types of peg lists. Following are some examples you can use to expand the above peg list beyond 20.

PEGGING EXERCISE #2: RHYMING PEG LIST

For numbers 21 through 30, select a word that rhymes with the second digit in the number. Of the 10 examples below, notice that half of the associations feature action words (e.g., run, ski, dive). Action is the "glue" that holds your picture together; it helps your picture tell a story. The story will be even easier to remember if you put yourself into the picture, as well.

Number	Picture Word	Association
21	Run	Run rhymes with one
22	Glue	Glue rhymes with two
23	Ski	Ski rhymes with three
24	Door	Door rhymes with four
25	Dive	Dive rhymes with five
26	Mix	Mix rhymes with six
27	Kevin (Costner)	Kevin rhymes with seven
28	Plate	Plate rhymes with eight
29	Twine	Twine rhymes with nine
30	Dirty (clothes)	Dirty rhymes with thirty

PEGGING EXERCISE #3: BODY PEG LIST

Another type of peg list associates numbers with parts of the body—from toe to head. What makes this system more memorable is the way you go about learning the list. Stand and point to the corresponding body part while saying the number aloud. Imagine that the number is literally connected to the corresponding body part. Using movement and imagination along with your voice makes the list easier to remember. Try this technique to learn the next 10 peg words below.

Number	Picture Word	Association
31	Toes	"31" connected to toes
32	Shins	"32" connected to shins
33	Knees	"33" connected to knees
34	Thighs	"34" connected to thighs
35	Rear	"35" connected to rear
36	Waist	"36" connected to waist
37	Shoulders	"37" connected to shoulders
38	Neck	"38" connected to neck
39	Chin	"39" connected to chin
40	Head	"40" connected to head

PEGGING EXERCISE #4: ROOM PEG LIST

You can use a room in your house or workplace to build your peg list to 50. Select any room and visualize, from left to right, the placement of furniture, appliances, and other items. If you want to add more numbers onto your peg list, use other rooms. Again, imagine that the number is attached to the object in your room that you are associating it with. (For example, if you enter your kitchen and the first object to your left is a telephone, then the number 41 would be assigned to telephone, 42 to desk [the next object in the room], etc.) This method, also called loci, was developed by the Greeks thousands of years ago to help them remember ideas based on fixed positions or locations. Keep in mind that the list that follows is from my kitchen; your room list, of course, will be different.

Number	Picture Word	Association
41	Telephone	"41" connected to phone telephone
42	Desk	"42" connected to desk
43	Refrigerator	"43" connected to refrigerator
44	Pantry	"44" connected to pantry
45	Stove	"45" connected to stove
46	Sink	"46" connected to sink
47	Trash Can	"47" connected to trash can
48	Wine Rack	"48" connected to wine rack
49	Back Door	"49" connected to back door
50	Table	"50" connected to table

Notice the differences between the various peg lists. The logic list has stronger associations than the other lists, although the rhyme list also is strong because the words sound like the numbers they are associated with. The body and room lists may seem more random but can also be committed to memory with a little mental work. Regardless of the technique you use, pegging allows you to give meaning to abstract numbers. You can use the above peg lists, or think up ones of your own. Most people learn their own peg lists faster than someone else's because the process of "creating" makes a deeper memory impression. Regardless of whose peg list you use, commit it to long-term memory by visualizing each number with its association as solidly as possible.

PEGGING EXERCISE #5: PRACTICING YOUR LOGIC PEG LIST

Once you've locked your peg lists into your long-term memory, it is time to put them to work. Let's say you need to pick up five items at the grocery store. Using absurd visualizations, connect each item you need to buy with the pictures you've pegged to numbers 1–5 on the logic list. Here is an example:

Logic List	Shopping Item	Visualization
1. Pencil	Lettuce	The eraser on your pencil is a head of lettuce that shreds as you erase something.
2. Faucet	Milk	You turn on a faucet and milk pours out, splashing all over you.

3. Triangle	Hot dogs	You are holding a triangle made out of hot dogs.
4. Table	Eggs	You are leaning on a table with legs that are eggs glued end to end, and the table smashes to the floor.
5. Fingers	Butter	You can't wiggle your fingers because they're made of sticks of butter, or Butterfingers candy bars.

Without looking back at your shopping list, close your book and see if you can recall the five items you need at the store.

Complete the shopping list below using the rest of the logic peg list. Be sure you've first committed the peg list to memory, otherwise attempting to peg new information onto your list will be an exercise in frustration. For each new item on your shopping list, visualize an absurd way to associate it with the permanent item on your peg list. If you add action to your mental image, it will be easier to remember.

Logic List	Shopping Item	Your Visualization
6. Beer	Laundry Detergent	_____
7. Dice	Steak	_____
8. Skate	Soap	_____
9. Cat	Orange Juice	_____
10. Indians	Bread	_____
11. Ladder	Corn Flakes	_____
12. Bread Rolls	Cucumbers	_____
13. Ghost	Spaghetti	_____
14. Gold Ring	Ice Cream	_____
15. Tax Forms	Chicken	_____
16. Candles	Bacon	_____
17. Car	Rice	_____
18. Flag	Tuna	_____
19. Golf Shoes	Pickles	_____
20. Money	Peanuts	_____

The biggest challenge faced by most beginning peg list users is creating illogical pictures in their mind's eye. If you are unsure whether a mental image is absurd enough, ask yourself, "Could this happen in real life?" If the answer is "yes," or even "maybe," your association may not be ridiculous enough to stick in your memory. With practice you will get better at creating memorable visualizations. There are no "right" or "wrong" images. The images you conjure up will be the best possible memory tools for you because they are your inventions. This is the kind of thinking that poets, painters, musical composers, inventors, and other creative people use on a regular basis. They stretch and exaggerate their ideas and make unexpected associations all the time. By looking at the world from different perspectives, they let their imaginations soar. Remember, Einstein invented his theory of relativity when he visualized himself riding on a beam of light!

PEGGING EXERCISE #6: PRACTICING YOUR RHYMING PEG LIST

Let's try to remember five more grocery items, this time using 21–25 of the Rhyme Peg List. As with the other peg lists, the Rhyme List must first be committed to memory in order to be useful. Remember to associate each new item in an exaggerated or nonsensical way to the existing item on your list. Make each visualization as vivid as you can, using action images wherever possible.

Rhyme List	Shopping Item	Your Visualization
21. Run	Roast Beef	_____
22. Glue	Cheese	_____
23. Ski	Apple	_____
24. Door	Baked Beans	_____
25. Dive	Brownie Mix	_____

PEGGING EXERCISE #7: PRACTICING YOUR BODY PEG LIST

Now, continue the exercise using the Body Peg List. Here are five more shopping items to give you practice with the Body List.

Body List	Shopping Item	Your Visualization
31. Toes	Pears	_____
32. Shins	Pancakes	_____

33. Knees	Grapes	_____
34. Thighs	Ground beef	_____
35. Rear	Fish	_____

PEGGING EXERCISE #8: PRACTICING YOUR ROOM PEG LIST

Next, create your own Room Peg List by selecting a room in your home and assigning the placement of objects in that room to the numbers below. If the first object you see on the left when you enter your room is a sofa, then sofa would be 41. (Note that it is easier to assign numbers to objects from left to right or right to left in your room.) Once you've memorized your room list, fill in the blanks below.

Room List	Shopping Item	Your Visualization
41._____	Vinegar	_____
42._____	Coffee cake	_____
43._____	Toothpaste	_____
44._____	Vitamins	_____
45._____	Olives	_____
46._____	Mouthwash	_____
47._____	Sponge	_____
48._____	Tangerines	_____
49._____	Pantyhose	_____
50._____	TV Dinners	_____

USES FOR PEG LISTS

A grocery list is but one of many uses for peg lists. Here are some others:

- "To do" lists
- Speeches and presentations
- Reading material
- Information on tests and exams
- Information at meetings and lectures
- Appointments
- Dates

- Times
- Numbers
- Learning New Languages
- Learning Vocabulary

IMAGINATION AND EXAGGERATION

Throughout history, people have always told each other stories. With each telling, a story tends to get a little more exaggerated; it grows farther and farther from the truth. It is natural to exaggerate a story in order to make it funnier or more interesting. This natural tendency can be put to good use when it comes to enhancing your memory through techniques such as visualization. You can get better at using your imagination just by letting yourself go. Pretend you are a child again. Make up stories and events. Exaggerate or blow the story out of proportion. Have fun doing the exercise below, using the creative side of your brain.

EXERCISE 3-3: IMAGINATION WITH EXAGGERATION

In the spaces below, use your imagination to create stories based on the following scenarios:

1. You captured the world's most dangerous animal.

_____

_____

_____

_____

_____

_____

_____

_____

Continued on next page

2. You saved the world from certain disaster.

_____

_____

_____

_____

_____

_____

_____

3. You took a magic pill that shrunk you to the size of a peanut.

_____

_____

_____

_____

_____

_____

_____

4. You won the Nobel Prize for an extraordinary discovery.

_____

_____

_____

_____

_____

_____

_____

_____

USING VISUALIZATION AND ASSOCIATION TO REMEMBER NAMES

There is no sound sweeter than a person's own name.

–Dale Carnegie

The inability to remember people's names is probably the most common complaint we in the memory education field hear from our students/participants. The cost of forgetting a name can carry a high price, both socially and professionally. It therefore makes sense to invest time and energy to overcome this problem.

Why do so many people have trouble remembering names? Many people attribute their forgetfulness to inattention, not caring, or being distracted—and they may be partially right. However, the overriding reason most names are difficult to retain is because they are abstract and therefore have no meaning to us. Notice I said *most* names. All names, first names and surnames, can be separated into two major categories: Names that evoke immediate, inherent images upon hearing them, and names that are abstract and conjure up no universal image. The following names at the top of the next page fall into the first category.

First Names	Surnames
Art	Cook
Matt	Brown
John	Carpenter
Glen	Baker
Georgia	Goodman

Here are some abstract names from the second category:

First Names	Surnames
Elaine	Conti
Christine	Smolensky
Arlene	Morgan
Louise	McGuire
Fred	Moreno
Scott	Littman

Although these names seem intangible, with a little imagination, they can be made more concrete. In fact, virtually every abstract name, no matter how strange it sounds, can be substituted with a like-sounding word or words that are easy to visualize or associate with something tangible. You can do this by finding a word or phrase that rhymes or sounds similar to the name, or you can break down the abstract name into syllables in order to create a picture in your mind. "Minnesota" might become "mini soda;" "Ruth" might be associated with a Baby Ruth candy bar; "Mike" can be pictured holding a microphone (or having a head shaped like a microphone). Borrowing from the list above, Scott Littman could become a "cot" that is "lit" up by a "man" holding a match. The very act of coming up with substitute words forces you to concentrate on a person's name more intensely than you would otherwise. This also aids in memory. Here are some more examples of how this works:

> Bernice = burn knee   Mr. Rosen = Mr. Rose Inn
>
> Kathleen = cat lean   Ms. Tucker = Ms. Trucker or Tuck her (in)

EXERCISE 3-5: CREATING FIRST NAME PICTURES

Create a mental picture for each of the following first names and write it in the space provided. You may use a rhyming word or substitute word that is representative or symbolic of the name. In some cases, you may need to break the name down into syllables to get your pictures.

1. Al = <u>Example: Owl or Al Capone</u>

2. Nicole = _____

3. Art = _____

4. Jean = _____

5. Fred = _____

6. James = _____

7. Carl = _____

8. Dan = _____

9. Anthony = _____

10. Debbie = _____

EXERCISE 3-6: CREATING SURNAME PICTURES

Create a mental picture for each of the following surnames and write it in the spaces provided. You may use a rhyming word or substitute word that is representative or symbolic of the name. Again, it may help to also break the name down into syllables.

1. Atwater = <u>Example: At the water</u>

2. Carmichael = _____

3. Crawford = _____

Continued on next page

4. Hawkins = _____

5. Jarrett = _____

6. Rabinowicz = _____

7. Schuster = _____

8. Shelton = _____

9. Olsen = _____

10. Sherman = _____

REMEMBERING NAMES USING SIGHT PEGS

It is the common wonder of all men, how among so many millions of faces there should be none alike.

– Sir Thomas Browne

Visualizing a name concretely in your mind's eye is only the first step in the process of improving your memory for names. The second step is associating your visualization with the person's physical appearance in an absurdly memorable way. This is done by use of sight pegs. There are two kinds of sight pegs: temporary and permanent. A temporary sight peg is something transient about a person's appearance, such as an article of clothing or piece of jewelry. The best temporary sight peg is always the first transient thing you notice about a person (e.g., an unusual necktie). A permanent sight peg is an outstanding physical feature or anything else that doesn't change, such as a large nose, protruding ears, blue eyes, dimples, a scar, baldness, and the like. Again, it is helpful to use the first feature that strikes you about a person.

Temporary sight pegs provide greater flexibility since there are infinite variations in how people dress and accessorize. Permanent sight pegs are fewer in number but may help you remember the person the next time you meet.

Here are some examples of how temporary and permanent sight pegs can force names to stick in your memory:

1. Name: Harry

    Mental image suggested by name: Harry turns into Hairy

    Temporary sight peg: Harry's bow tie (first thing noticed)

    Connection: Harry wearing a big, hairy bow tie (make it as descriptive as possible, such as long, red hair, neatly parted, growing out of the tie, etc.)

2. Name: Judith

    Mental image suggested by name: Judith sounds like "chewed it"

    Permanent Sight Peg: Large teeth

    Connection: Judith eating something crunchy, her large teeth chewing it into tiny morsels

Using temporary and permanent sight pegs to remember names takes practice, but it can be fun. Most people find it easier to start off with the temporary sight-peg technique. Identifying permanent sight pegs requires keen observation skills; locking into features is the most challenging part of the name-face association process. At first, you may feel uncomfortable choosing an outstanding physical feature, especially when it is on someone you like, respect, or are intimidated by (such as a new supervisor at work). If you are having trouble identifying permanent sight pegs, pretend you need to describe the person to a police sketch artist. In time, you will become more adept at observing people.

MEMORY CHECK

In the space below, jot down the most important points you learned from Part Three.

_____

_____

_____

_____

_____

_____

_____

_____

_____

_____

_____

_____

_____

_____

_____

_____

_____

_____

_____

Get a jump-start on memory fitness by "aerobicizing" your mind!

FundaMENTAL #5

Adopt a Lifestyle of Physical Fitness

LET'S GET PHYSICAL

When we talk about health, we must consider both physical and mental well-being. You can't really be in good physical shape without being in good mental shape, and vice versa. Because a sound body fosters a sound mind and better memory, Part Four focuses on exercise and diet.

FundaMENTAL #5: Adopt a Lifestyle of Physical Fitness

Body and mind are closely related and mental efficiency
is affected by the state of the body.

– Harry Maddox

The fact that physical activity benefits the mind as well as the body is backed by scientific studies. Research suggests, for example, that regular exercise may alleviate certain symptoms of mild to moderate depression and anxiety, and make you better able to cope psychologically with stress. Studies have shown that exercise can also increase your academic performance, confidence, emotional stability, self-control, concentration, work efficiency, and, of course, memory.

Clearly, physical fitness is a state of body <u>and</u> mind. It improves your appearance, posture, agility, sleep patterns, endurance, energy, heart, lungs, and blood vessels, immune system, and recuperative powers. And all of these add up to a healthier, longer, and more enjoyable mental and physical life. Be sure to check with your doctor before beginning any exercise program.

EXERCISE 4-1: EVALUATING YOUR FITNESS LEVEL

1. Does your body feel or look tense?   Yes   No

2. Do you have excess fat on your hips, arms, or thighs?   Yes   No

3. Are parts of your body too thin?   Yes   No

4. Does exertion leave you stiff with aching muscles?   Yes   No

Continued on next page

---

5. Do you become breathless easily?   Yes   No

6. Are you 20 pounds over or underweight?   Yes   No

7. Are you able to stretch without straining or aching?   Yes   No

8. Does your abdomen bulge or sag?   Yes   No

9. Do you have problems sleeping?   Yes   No

10. Are you overly susceptible to minor aches and illnesses?   Yes   No

11. Do you have good posture?   Yes   No

12. Do you have difficulty walking up stairs, bending, lifting, or getting in and out of chairs or cars?   Yes   No

If you answered "Yes" to more than five questions, you probably need to exercise more.

EXERCISE 4-2: SELF-ASSESSMENT: HOW ACTIVE IS YOUR LIFESTYLE?

Place a check next to each activity that you engage in, and circle how often you do the activity each week. Add any other activities in which you engage during the week. Your ratings indicate how active your lifestyle is.

Activity/Exercise	How Many Times Per Week?						
___ Hiking	1	2	3	4	5	6	7
___ Swimming	1	2	3	4	5	6	7
___ Skiing	1	2	3	4	5	6	7
___ Tennis	1	2	3	4	5	6	7
___ Basketball	1	2	3	4	5	6	7
___ Golf	1	2	3	4	5	6	7
___ Roller Blading	1	2	3	4	5	6	7

Continued on next page

___ Walking	1	2	3	4	5	6	7
___ Jogging	1	2	3	4	5	6	7
___ Aerobic Dancing	1	2	3	4	5	6	7
___ Weight-Lifting	1	2	3	4	5	6	7
___ Volleyball	1	2	3	4	5	6	7
___ Badminton	1	2	3	4	5	6	7
___ Dancing	1	2	3	4	5	6	7
___ Racquetball	1	2	3	4	5	6	7
___ Rowing	1	2	3	4	5	6	7
___ Bicycling	1	2	3	4	5	6	7
___ Stretching	1	2	3	4	5	6	7
___ Table Tennis	1	2	3	4	5	6	7
_____	1	2	3	4	5	6	7
_____	1	2	3	4	5	6	7
_____	1	2	3	4	5	6	7

At this time, there are no scientifically backed guidelines on how much exercise you need to improve your memory. Some studies have attempted to find out, but there have been no conclusive findings. In general, however, the more active you are, the better off your mind and memory will be, according to researchers in the mind sciences field.

EXERCISE 4-3: QUIZ: WHAT'S YOUR EXERCISE IQ?

Mark the following statements true or false (T or F).

_____ 1. Exercise means making yourself fit.

Continued on next page

_____ 2. You can use exercise to cleanse your mind.

_____ 3. American adults are more physically active than they were 200 years ago.

_____ 4. There is preliminary evidence that exercise can relieve depression.

_____ 5. Exercise should be sustained for 45 minutes to an hour in order to be effective.

_____ 6. Climbing stairs requires more energy per minute than traditional exercises such as swimming and jogging.

_____ 7. There is no such thing as too much exercise.

_____ 8. Consistency is the most important element in becoming and staying fit.

_____ 9. You can get fit by being active.

_____ 10. The time needed for satisfactory warm-up varies from person to person.

_____ 11. It is better to exercise in the morning as opposed to the afternoon.

_____ 12. The more you know about fitness, the more motivation you will have to exercise.

Answers

1. *False*. Just because you are exercising doesn't mean you are getting fit. You must work hard enough to break a sweat for at least 20 minutes three times a week in order to improve your level of aerobic fitness. To burn more fat, you must do aerobic exercise for 30 to 45 minutes three or more times a week.

2. *True*. After exercise, most people feel that their minds are less cluttered and more focused. In a sense, working out your body gives your mind a rest.

3. *False*. Before automobiles and televisions, Americans did far more walking and physical labor than they do today. In general, technology and automation have made us lazier.

4. *True*. Research has shown that clinical depression improved significantly in men and women who exercised three or four times a week for eight to ten consecutive weeks.

5. *False*. Exercise need not be continuous to have an impact. You can accumulate 30 to 45 minutes of exercise throughout your day by cutting the grass with a push mower and walking to the store instead of driving.

6. *True*. Climbing stairs is a great way to exercise. Whenever possible, use the stairs instead of an escalator or elevator.

7. *False*. Too much exercise can suppress the immune system, leaving you more susceptible to colds and other infections. Exercising intensely for more than two hours at a stretch can also lead to fatigue and raise your risk for injury. Women who exercise too much on a chronic basis can suffer hormonal changes that cause them to stop ovulating.

8. *True*. In order to exercise regularly, look for a fitness program you can use in any environment. For example, walking two miles every day can be done in your neighborhood, in a shopping mall when it is raining outside, on a treadmill in a gym, at home, or in a hotel when you are traveling.

9. *False*. There is more to being fit than most people think. Many people who are active in a variety of sports, such as tennis, golf, and skiing, believe they are in good shape but may be unable to touch their toes or jump rope for a minute. Diet and other factors, such as strength and endurance, also play important roles in fitness.

10. *True*. Experts recommend a warm-up period of 5 to 15 minutes. How long you need to warm up depends on how fast it takes your body to loosen up and break a sweat. Temperature also plays a role. As a rule, the colder the weather, the longer your warm-up should be.

11. *False*. It doesn't matter what time of day you exercise, as long as you do it. The best time to exercise is when it fits into your schedule on a consistent basis.

12. *True*. Motivating yourself to exercise regularly is the key. Aim to make exercise a part of your daily life. If you exercise properly and consistently, you will eventually see results. It is those results—a leaner body and sharper mind—that will motivate you to continue with your exercise program.

(CAUTION: If you suffer an exercise injury, rest the injured part of your body until it is healed. Never try to exercise through pain. And again, before beginning any exercise program, check with your doctor.)

MAXIMIZING YOUR FITNESS LEVEL

For maximum energy and fitness, it is important to follow an exercise program that includes both aerobic and strength-training activities, such as sit-ups and lifting weights. Gentle stretching is also helpful to increase your flexibility and decrease your risk of injury. Here are some specific suggestions that can boost your physical energy:

- Add Yoga stretches to your aerobic exercise program. Yoga is particularly useful for people who work in high-stress environments.

- Find the right amount of exercise for your lifestyle. Too much or too little exercise can cause fatigue. Consistent, moderate exercise is better for your body and your well-being.

- For exercise beginners, walking is best. You can add other activities, such as swimming, cycling, or aerobic dancing later. Build up your energy level gradually to avoid injury.

- Examine how your eating and sleeping habits fit into your daily schedule. Your body and mind respond best to regularity. Regular eating and sleeping schedules will help you maintain a regular exercise schedule.

- Exercise at your aerobic capacity. Ultimately, you should be able to sustain an aerobic exercise for at least 30 minutes without getting breathless. After a while, a regular exercise program will enable your heart and lungs to work more efficiently. The blood supply to your muscles will improve, and your blood volume will increase. By improving your body's capacity to bring in oxygen and deliver it to your cells, you are boosting your energy. Your sleeping, eating, and digestion patterns will improve, and you will feel better emotionally. In addition, aerobic exercise accelerates your metabolism, which means you burn calories faster during exercise and at rest.

HOW MUCH EXERCISE IS NEEDED? Just how much exercise will keep your body, mind, and memory in peak condition? Many experts say we don't need as much exercise as previously thought to derive health benefits. How much exercise you need depends on your personal fitness goals. Those goals may include improved heart and lung function, increased muscular strength, more endurance, a leaner body, or increased flexibility. An effective exercise program should include a careful balance of activities that suits your needs. Doing the exercise regularly is more important than trying to kill yourself at every workout. For example, running for 45 minutes three or four times a week is not for everyone. If you want exercise to produce lasting benefits, it needs to become a lifelong habit. Your motivation level will be higher if you select activities you enjoy. If you don't like to jog, don't do it; walk instead, or do something else you enjoy.

You can start by setting some short-term fitness goals that can be measured. Charting your progress will help motivate you. Noting positive changes will keep you going during the critical first three months that it takes to incorporate exercise into your daily life. You can also set long-term exercise goals for 6, 9, or 12 months. This will also help you understand how long it takes to see results. Losing fat and gaining strength and endurance don't happen overnight.

10 WAYS TO FOSTER A COMMITMENT TO FITNESS

Gradually build your activity level. Excess can cause injury, and you'll be more likely to drop out. Here are some ways to help foster a commitment to fitness.

- *Make exercise a priority in your schedule.* Not having enough time to exercise is a convenient excuse. We always can make time for what we think is important.
- *Make exercising convenient.* Don't join a health spa miles from your home or workplace. If you prefer to exercise outdoors, have an indoor exercise setup for inclement weather.
- *Try not to miss too many workout sessions.* Missing on occasion won't hurt, but skipping too many successive workouts will take away what you've worked hard to achieve thus far.
- *Set realistic fitness goals for your body type.* You don't necessarily need to keep intensifying your program once you have met your fitness goals. At that point, you can maintain fitness with less activity.
- *Be prepared to accept temporary setbacks.* An illness, injury, or personal crisis will inevitably interrupt your workout schedule. Pick up your regimen as soon as you can.

- *Build a network of exercise support.* Talk to others who exercise. Read articles and books about fitness. Allow yourself to be inspired by other people's accomplishments.

- *Work on other health changes.* If you are overweight or you smoke, let exercise be a catalyst for change. Set all-around health goals.

- *Consider competing.* You may get motivated by training for a race, swim meet, or tennis match. Keep the competition in proper perspective, though; it's the training and preparation, rather than the winning, that's most important.

- *Reward yourself.* Treat yourself to a movie or new clothes once you've achieved your fitness goals.

LIFESTYLE CHANGES

Even if you don't exercise regularly, you can still incorporate enough physical activity into your daily routine to keep your large muscle groups toned. Physical activity is anything that gets the muscles moving over a period of time. It can be occupational, recreational, or vocational. Any physical activity brings more oxygen to the brain, which helps keep the mind youthful and agile. The idea is to move your body, get your blood circulating, and shake up those old and new memories.

Lifestyle changes need not be drastic or major. They begin by, as Stephen Blair, director of epidemiology at the Cooper Institute for Aerobic Research in Dallas, says, getting people off the couch. Here are a few suggestions:

- Walk up escalators instead of riding them
- Park a little farther away from the mall
- Use part of your lunch hour to walk (be sure to walk fast enough to elevate your heart rate)
- Cut the lawn, garden, and rake leaves
- Clean the whole house at one time

PHYSICAL AND MENTAL ENERGY

Energy is both mental and physical. The mind and body are interrelated, so if the body suffers, the mind will also suffer. Let's take a closer look at the interplay of mental and physical energy.

MENTAL ENERGY. Some people refer to mental energy as "get-up-and-go," zest, drive, enthusiasm, or vigor. Regardless of how you label it, mental energy gives you the ambition you need to tackle anything. At times, our mental energy flow can wane or become a little erratic. Daydreaming is one clue that this is happening; another is talking yourself into skipping an exercise session. Fortunately, there are ways to reinvigorate your mental energy.

Following are some reasons people lag mentally and some mental energy boosters that can help:

- **Problem**: Mental fatigue. **Booster**: Make some small changes in your life. Read something different, study a new language, take up a new sport, or learn a new skill.

- **Problem**: Feeling overwhelmed by the hustle-bustle of daily life. **Booster**: Give yourself time to escape your normal routine. Take a walk in the woods, go sailing, or read a book on the beach—whatever makes you feel good.

- **Problem**: Boredom. **Booster**: Find a challenge. Challenge yourself to meet a new friend. Ask for a new responsibility at work. Help someone else solve a problem. Take a spur-of-the-moment vacation. These are just a few ways to make life more interesting and get you out of a rut.

- **Problem**: Feeling non-creative. **Booster**: Do some creative thinking. Practice some memory techniques that require imagination and visualization. Or create something tangible such as writing a story or drawing a picture. Nothing makes you feel more alive than getting your creative juices flowing.

- **Problem**: Feeling depressed or useless. **Booster**: Shed negative thoughts and replace them with positive ones. Positive thoughts create positive energy. Turn "I think I can't" into "I think I can."

- **Problem**: Feeling useless or helpless. **Booster**: Remind yourself of all the things you can do and change; believe in your ability to do so. Being overly self-critical can zap your mental energy. Don't let others drain your energy by controlling and coercing you. Recognize that you are in control of your own life.

- **Problem**: Feeling unable to reach your goals. **Booster**: Visualize what you want to achieve. Imagining what you want will give you the mental energy and focus to attain it. Another method is writing out your hopes and dreams and displaying them in your office or bedroom.

- **Problem**: Feeling emotionally detached from your work. **Booster**: Find a way to absorb yourself in whatever you are doing. Engulfing yourself in your work will keep your energy levels high.

- **Problem**: Feeling stressed out. **Booster**: Take time to meditate. Setting a few minutes aside each day for quiet reflection can restore the mind naturally and build energy reserves.

- **Problem**: Being disorganized. **Booster:** Create a work station compatible with your mental energy needs. For example, put everything in its proper place by creating and using a filing system, and keep track of your schedule by using a calendar.

- **Problem**: Feeling overworked. **Booster**: Give your mind a break every 90 minutes. Take a brisk, five-minute walk outside, if possible.

FOOD FOR THOUGHT

There are times when your mental acuity must operate at peak efficiency. Just ask a student who is taking a final exam, a businesswoman arguing her case for a promotion, a technician trying to grasp new skills, or an executive making an important decision. In this section, you will learn how food can increase your energy and ability to concentrate in order to remember.

HIGH ACHIEVEMENT EATING. Judith Wurtman, Ph.D., a researcher at the Massachusetts Institute of Technology, has offered the following guidelines to help keep you in top mental form for sustained concentration and focus:

1. Avoid high-fat, high-calorie foods when you need to be at your mental peak. For your mind to be at its clearest and sharpest, your brain must be richly supplied with blood, not losing it due to competition from your digestive tract.

2. Include more protein in your breakfast and lunch. Protein switches on the "alertness" chemicals in the brain. One high-protein breakfast food is egg whites. Lunch-time protein can come from meats, poultry, or seafood, including tuna fish.

3. Avoid alcohol prior to any learning session or anytime you need to be at your peak energy level.

4. Avoid consuming more caffeine than you are accustomed to. Having two or three cups of coffee the morning before a training class when you are used to one cup, for instance, could be overstimulating and distracting, which will make it difficult to concentrate.

5. Eat carbohydrates, such as pasta and breads, to unwind and relax toward the end of the day.

EXERCISE 4-4: FOOD, ENERGY, AND DIGESTION

Read the following and determine if each statement is true or false (T or F). Answers can be found below.

_____ 1. Blood leaves the brain after you eat, making you more lethargic.

_____ 2. To sustain your energy level, consume foods or beverages that contain processed or refined sugar.

_____ 3. Pork and beef take the longest time to digest.

_____ 4. Your emotions can affect your memory.

_____ 5. Fruit and vegetables take a relatively long time to digest.

_____ 6. White flour causes other foods to move through the digestive tract at a slower rate.

_____ 7. Turkey is rich in tryptophan, an amino acid that can make you tired and sleepy.

_____ 8. Caffeine jump-starts your brain processes but can also make you jittery.

_____ 9. Alcohol can slow down your thinking.

_____ 10. Because alcohol reduces stress, it can aid your memory.

Answers

1. *True*. For example, blood leaves the brain when the digestive system needs it to break down food.

2. *False*. Refined sugar creates only a temporary burst of energy.

3. *True*. Pork takes 48 hours to completely break down; after that comes beef, poultry, fish, vegetables and fruit, in descending order.

4. *True*. Food affects your moods; you can feel energized or lethargic, depending on what you eat, when you eat, and how much you eat.

5. *False*. Owing to their high water content, fruits and vegetables are digested faster than other foods.

6. *True*. White processed flour, when mixed with liquid, will become like paste, which slows down the movement of blood and oxygen through your system.

7. *True*. Tryptophan is an amino acid that will produce a relaxed state of mind.

8. *True*. Caffeine is a stimulant that can shorten your attention span if used in excess.

9. *True*. Alcohol is a depressant that can produce a calming affect.

10. *False*. Although alcohol does relax you and reduce stress, it also slows down your reflexes and thought processes. And excessive long-term use can be devastating on the brain.

VITAMINS, HERBS, AND MEMORY

Despite their controversy in the United States, vitamin supplements and medicinal herbs have been used in China and Europe for centuries. While most are used to relieve physical ailments, a number of vitamins and at least one herb have been linked to memory function and overall mental state.

THIAMIN (VITAMIN B1). Without thiamin, the brain and nervous system would collapse. Its primary role is to help convert carbohydrates into energy. Symptoms of mild thiamin deficiency may include irritability, depression, lack of initiative, insomnia, and inability to concentrate. Severe thiamin deficiency can actually erase long-term memories. It is easy to overlook or misdiagnose a thiamin deficiency because its symptoms can be vague, particularly during the early stages. Thiamin is found in whole-wheat products. Pork, liver, and peas are also good sources. Many flour and grain products in the United States are fortified with thiamin.

RIBOFLAVIN. Riboflavin is an essential nutrient that plays a role in controlling energy production from glucose in the brain and nervous system. Riboflavin helps to convert the foods we eat into energy. It is available in meats, fish, whole-grain products, milk products, vegetables, and foods fortified with B vitamins.

NIACIN. Niacin helps red blood cells carry oxygen to the brain. Senility (or dementia) can set in when there is a niacin deficiency. Niacin can also lower your cholesterol level and is therefore frequently recommended, along with exercise and a low-fat diet, to people with heart disease. Like riboflavin, niacin helps living cells generate energy from food. Niacin also eliminates pellagra, a deficiency disease that could lead to mental impairment. Foods rich in niacin include beets, chicken, fish, peanuts, pork, sunflower seeds, turkey, and veal.

CHOLINE. Choline is an essential dietary component found in a wide variety of meats and vegetables. Choline is considered a vitamin by some nutritionists (it's included in many of the more complete B vitamin supplements). Choline-rich foods include ham, trout, brussels sprouts, oatmeal, soybeans, cabbage, cauliflower, kale, lettuce, and potatoes. Your body can manufacture additional choline, provided you maintain a well-balanced diet. Choline has a moderate memory-enhancement effect. Scientists are still testing this nutrient's potential impact on memory impairment in the elderly.

LECITHIN. Lecithin is a type of fat. Maintaining high levels of lecithin helps you think more quickly and efficiently. People with high IQs tend to have large amounts of this substance in their brains. To increase your memory power, eat lecithin-rich foods such as soybeans, meats, eggs, and wheat germ. Lecithin supplements are available in most health-food stores, although most dietitians recommend getting nutrients through foods, not supplements.

SELENIUM. When combined with Vitamin E, selenium enhances the parts of the brain associated with memory. Many people are deficient in selenium and do not realize it. To ensure you are getting enough selenium, eat plenty of wheat germ, wheat bran, rice, broccoli, cabbage, celery, chicken, cucumbers, onions, mushrooms, and dairy products.

GINGKO BILOBA. Gingko Biloba, an herb, helps increase the amount of oxygen that reaches your brain to make you more alert. This herb has been used in China and Europe for centuries and is extracted from the leaves of the Gingko tree. It is available in most health-food stores and can be taken in capsules or made into tea.

(CAUTION: Before taking any vitamin supplements or herbs, consult your physician or a nutritionist.)

MEMORY CHECK

In the space below, write down the most important points you learned from Part Four.

_____

_____

_____

_____

_____

_____

_____

_____

_____

_____

_____

_____

_____

_____

_____

_____

_____

_____

_____

PART FIVE

MEETING YOUR MEMORY CHALLENGES HEAD-ON

The difference between a successful person and others is not a lack of strength, not a lack of knowledge, but rather a lack of will.

– Author Unknown

Your Memory Improvement Plan

Now that you have learned how to improve your memory, it's time to take action by developing a Memory Improvement Plan. Give some thought to the information presented in this book and the feedback you received from its questionnaires, quizzes, and exercises. What have you learned about memory, in general, and your own memory attitudes, abilities, and skills? What can you do to improve your memory? The format below will help clarify your answers. (You may want to refer back to specific questionnaires and exercises where your skills were assessed.)

A. I have memory strengths in the following areas (e.g., visualization, observation):

Area 1 _____

Area 2 _____

Area 3 _____

Area 4 _____

B. I need to work on the following areas to improve my memory (e.g., concentration, negative self-concept about memory potential):

Area 1 _____

Area 2 _____

Area 3 _____

Area 4 _____

C. For each area of weakness listed in Part B above, describe immediate and long-term action steps you will take to improve. For instance, if Area 1 is difficulty concentrating, some immediate action steps could be removing yourself from distractions when possible, asking yourself questions to stay focused, and listening with the intent of reporting the information to a third party. Long-term action steps might include reading two new books on listening and concentrating (see Bibliography), searching the Internet for resources on the subject of concentration, or taking a course or workshop on listening/memory.

Area 1—Immediate Action Steps:

a. _____

b. _____

c. _____

d. _____

Long-term Action Steps:

a. _____

b. _____

c. _____

d. _____

Area 2—Immediate Action Steps:

a. _____

b. _____

c. _____

d. _____

Long-term Action Steps:

a. _____

b. _____

c. _____

d. _____

Area 3—Immediate Action Steps:

a. _____

b. _____

c. _____

d. _____

    Long-term Action Steps:

a. _____

b. _____

c. _____

d. _____

Area 4—Immediate Action Steps:

a. _____

b. _____

c. _____

d. _____

    Long-term Action Steps:

a. _____

b. _____

c. _____

d. _____

D. List obstacles that might get in the way of your improvement plan; then state your plan for overcoming these obstacles.

Obstacle	Plan to Overcome Obstacle
EXAMPLE:	EXAMPLE:
Too tired to concentrate	Talk to doctor or nutritionist to identify cause of fatigue; begin physical fitness program or take more breaks from work
1. _____	1. _____
	_____
	_____
2. _____	2. _____
	_____
	_____

E. List people who can help you follow your memory improvement plan and reach your memory goals. For each person, describe the kind of help they can give you.

Person   Help He/She Can Give You

EXAMPLE: EXAMPLE:
Spouse   Let me know immediately
                                          when I stop paying
                                          attention to what you're saying.

Co-Worker   Ask me questions from time
(identify by name)   to time to make sure I am
                                          understanding you correctly.

1. _____   1. _____
                                             _____
                                             _____

2. _____   2. _____
                                             _____
                                             _____

3. _____   3. _____
                                             _____
                                             _____

Tips At-A-Glance

Following is a quick-reference guide to memory aids. Many were covered in this book; others were not. Although some are common-sense, they are not always common practice. The "internal" tips are ones that you can do mentally. "External" tips involve taking some kind of physical action, such as writing something down.

INTERNAL MEMORY TIPS

1. Pay attention and concentrate on one thing at a time.

2. Actively listen and focus on what is being said.

3. Reduce or eliminate background/competing noises or distractions when possible.

4. Observe using all of your senses.

5. Keep a positive attitude about your memory abilities.

6. Relax; take periodic breaks from work.

7. Don't over complain about memory lapses; everyone has them.

8. Bolster your self-esteem by congratulating yourself on memory successes.

9. Be selective on what to remember and what to forget; it's okay not to remember everything.

10. Reminisce and discuss past experiences with others.

11. Visualize things you want to remember using exaggeration, humor, and action in an illogical way.

12. Laugh to break the tension of forgetting.

13. Think up an absurd story to remember a series of items.

14. Practice pegging and linking techniques whenever you have an opportunity to do so.

15. Use verbal repetition to store information in short-term memory.

16. Try the alphabet search (Does her name begin with A, B, C, etc.?).

17. Strive to understand something fully before trying to commit it to memory.

18. Ask questions to clarify and verify information.

19. Use verbal elaboration. When you learn something new, talk about it and teach others. This will enhance your comprehension and make it easier to remember.

20. Organize new information into groups or categories, by names, relationships, logical order, or levels of importance.

21. Find a way to be interested in something that you should be paying attention to but really don't care about.

22. Continue to test and challenge yourself; exercise your mind as much as possible.

23. Eat the right foods at the right times to optimize your energy level and ability to concentrate.

24. Use acronyms (first letters of each word) to remember a series of items (e.g., "HOMES" to remember the names of the Great Lakes: **H**uron, **O**ntario, **M**ichigan, **E**rie, **S**uperior).

25. Make up a sentence using the first letter of each word (e.g., **E**very **G**ood **B**oy **D**oes **F**ine to remember the musical scale EGBDF).

26. Make and listen to an audio tape of information you need to learn several times.

27. Remember an important date or number by associating it with a familiar date, such as an historic event, birthday, or graduation.

EXTERNAL MEMORY TIPS

1. Keep a calendar for appointments, and refer to it before making new plans.

2. Keep a list by the door of things to take with you when leaving.

3. Make a daily "To Do" list and prioritize items on the list.

4. Take notes; the act of writing will make a deeper memory impression.

5. Use both sides of your brain to remember (e.g., imagery and logic).

6. Change something in your environment to jog your memory (e.g., Hang clothes headed to the cleaners on your front door knob, or place a hammer on the table to remind yourself to hang a picture.).

7. Make a memory place in your home, one for objects such as keys and wallet that you use daily, and one for frequently used information, such as phone numbers, bills, insurance policies, etc.

8. Put objects you need to remember in clear view (e.g., Place your medicine near your toothbrush where you know you will see it.).

A FINAL NOTE

It takes time to get rid of old habits and practice new ways of thinking. Be patient with yourself. Memory improvements may not come overnight, but with practice, they will come. It is my firm belief that you can best accomplish your memory goals through self-assessment, using a variety of strategies and techniques, implementing an action plan for change, and by understanding how memory works. I hope that this book has given you enough information to give you a "HEAD-START." The rest is up to you.

BIBLIOGRAPHY

Bone, Diane, *The Business of Listening*. Los Altos, CA: Crisp Publications, Inc., 1988.

Brown, Alan S., *Maximizing Memory Power*. New York: John Wiley & Sons, Inc., 1987.

Burley-Allen, Madelyn, *Memory Skills In Business*. Los Altos, CA: Crisp Publications, Inc., 1988.

Buzan, Tony, *Use Your Perfect Memory*. New York: Plume, 1990.

Crook, Thomas, *How To Remember Names*. New York: First Harper Perennial, 1992.

Fogler, Janet and Stern, Lynn, *Improving Your Memory*. Baltimore, MD: The Johns Hopkins University Press, 1994.

Frender, Gloria, *Learning To Learn*. Nashville, TN: Incentive Publishing, 1990.

Gardner, Howard, *Frames of Mind*. New York: Basic Books, Inc., 1983.

Gordon, Barry, *Memory*. New York: Mastermedia Limited, 1995.

Haas, Robert, *Eat Smart, Think Smart*. New York: Harper Collins Publisher, 1994.

Higbee, Kenneth, *Your Memory*. New York: Paragon House, 1993.

Horn, Sam, *Concentration!* Menlo Park, CA: Crisp Publications, Inc., 1991.

Jackowski, Edward J., *Hold It! You're Exercising Wrong*. New York: Fireside, 1995.

Lapp, Danielle C., *Don't Forget*. New York: McGraw Hill, 1987.

LePoncin, Monique, *Brain Fitness*. New York: Random House, Inc., 1990.

Michaud, Ellen and Wild, Russell, *Boost Your Brain Power*. New York: MJF Books, 1991.

Minninger, Joan and Dugan, Eleanora, *Rapid Memory in 7 Days*. New York: A Perigee Book, 1994.

Podell, Richard, *Doctor, Why Am I So Tired?* New York: Ballantine Books, 1987.

Prevention Magazine, *The Complete Book of Vitamins*. Emmons, PA: Rodale Press, 1984.

Russell, Peter, *The Brain Book*. New York: E. P. Dutton, 1979.

Trudeau, Kevin, *Mega Memory*. New York: William Morrow and Company, Inc., 1995.

Vos Savant, Marilyn and Fleischer, Leonore, *Brain Building*. New York: Bantam Books, 1991.

West, Robin, *Memory Fitness over 40*. Gainesville, FL: Triad Publishing, 1985.

Wurtman, Judith J., with Danbrot, Margaret, *Managing Your Mind And Mood Through Food*. New York: Harper & Row Publishers, Inc., 1986.

Audio and Video Tapes

American Association of Retired Persons, "Memory, the Long and Short of It." Washington, DC: AARP Social Outreach and Support Program Department, 1990.

Bruschi, Phil, "Releasing Your Personal Memory Power." Yardville, NJ: MIND AEROBICS, 1996.

Bruschi, Phil, "Memory Fitness In The Later Years." Yardville, NJ: MIND AEROBICS, 1997.

Hilton, Hermine, "The Executive Memory Guide." New York: Simon & Schuster, 1989.

Robbins, Anthony, "Living Health." San Diego, CA: Robbins Research International, Inc., 1991.

Trudeau, Kevin, "Mega Memory." Chicago, IL: Nightingale Conant Corporation, 1992.

GLOSSARY

Aerobics Exercise vigorous enough to condition the cardiopulmonary system.

Association The connecting together of new information to information already existing in the memory.

Attention Deficit When you hear information but do not register it because you are focused on something else at the time.

Concentration Sustained attention necessary to ensure that memories are recorded.

Cue Any event, thought, picture, word, sound, or other stimuli that triggers the retrieval of information from long-term memory.

Divided Attention Focusing on more than one thing at a time.

Encoding The learning and storing of information in the brain.

Interference Anything that distracts you from concentrating on something else.

Linking Using visual imagery to learn a list of items in sequence by forming a chain of associations.

Loci A technique or method of remembering ideas based on a location or fixed position.

Long-term Memory The accumulation of information that is not present in conscious thought but is stored for potential recollection.

Memory The mental capacity to recall or recognize experiences or impressions.

Mind That aspect of a human being that feels, perceives, thinks, wills, and reasons.

MIND AEROBICS A system of mental conditioning designed to improve the mind and memory by actively exercising the brain.

Mnemonics Memory aids based on association.

Pegging Using visual imagery to associate anything you need to remember with images previously associated with numbers.

Recall A self-initiated search for information from long-term memory.

Recognition The perception of information as something you already know.

Repression The inability to retrieve a memory because it is too painful or embarrassing.

Retention Deficit Information is stored in long-term memory but is improperly registered or poorly organized, which makes the information difficult to retrieve.

Retrieval Bringing information from long-term memory to conscious thought.

Rote A way of moving information from short-term to long-term memory by sheer repetition, with or without attention to meaning.

Selective Attention Making a conscious decision to focus on or define what you want to remember, why, and for how long.

Sensory Referring to the five senses through which all information enters the brain.

Short-term Memory Conscious thought; the part of the brain that holds the very small amount of information you can pay attention to at any given moment.

Give your mind and memory a mental workout today!

"RELEASING YOUR PERSONAL MEMORY POWER"
(on two audio cassette tapes)

BENEFITS

◇ Improve your self-confidence about your mind and memory
◇ Build up your powers of attention and concentration
◇ Give your mind and memory a workout
◇ Use visualization and association
◇ Relate physical exercise to memory power
◇ Use may tips, techniques, and strategies for remembering

"MEMORY FITNESS IN THE LATER YEARS"
(on two audio cassette tapes)

BENEFITS

◇ Develop self-confidence about your memory
◇ Dispel myths about aging and memory
◇ Learn to remember dates, names, & numbers
◇ Learn what causes forgetfulness & how to get around it
◇ Identify memory changes with aging
◇ Learn how your memory really works
◇ Develop your own memory systems

Mind Aerobics: The FundaMENTALS
of Memory Fitness
(paperback book)

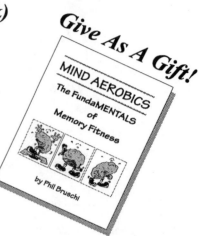

BENEFITS
Mind Aerobics is designed to enhance your memory by actively exercising the brain. Mental exercising is the key to unlocking enormous memory potential. This interactive book offers FundMENTALS that will motivate you to stretch beyond your present mental capabilities through the use of mind exercises, assessments, techniques, and strategies.

Quantity	Title	Price	Total
	"Releasing Your Personal Memory Power" (Audio Tapes)	$19.99	
	"Memory Fitness In the Later Years" (Audio Tapes)	$19.99	
	Mind Aerobics: The FundaMENTALS of Memory Fitness (Book)	$14.95	
	(NJ Residents add 6% sales tax)		
		Shipping	$3.00
		Amount of Total Order	

❑   I've enclosed a check or money order to Mind Aerobics or Phil Bruschi.

Name _____

Title (if applicable) _____

Company/Personal Address _____

City _____ State _____ Zip _____

Phone _____

Mail to: Phil Bruschi, P.O. Box 11233, Yardville, NJ 08620; Phone 609-581-8142